Praise for
UNCOMPARABLE

"Most advisors fight a never-ending battle to stand out as better than the rest. But as Kristen Luke so deftly illustrates, when you specialize in a niche, you instantly become 'the best' at winning those prospects . . . because there's no one to be compared to!"

—MICHAEL KITCES, Chief Financial Planning
Nerd, Kitces.com

"Kristen Luke has not just added to our vocabulary with the word 'uncomparable,' she has articulated the paradigm for advisor success in the coming decades."

—ROBERT HUEBSCHER, Founder, Advisor Perspectives

"A practical guide full of important information for advisors ready to enjoy the benefits of specializing their practice, complete with a three-year road map to make it happen. A great read for advisors ready to create more focused, efficient growth."

—STEPHANIE BOGAN, Founder, Limitless Advisor Coaching

UNCOMPARABLE

THE FINANCIAL ADVISOR'S GUIDE TO
STANDING OUT THROUGH NICHE MARKETING

KRISTEN LUKE

RIVER GROVE
BOOKS

Published by River Grove Books
Austin, TX
www.rivergrovebooks.com

Distributed by River Grove Books

Design and composition by Greenleaf Book Group
Cover design by Greenleaf Book Group

Publisher's Cataloging-in-Publication data is available.

Paperback ISBN: 978-1-63299-693-0

Hardcover ISBN: 978-1-63299-694-7

eBook ISBN: 978-1-63299-695-4

First Edition

This book is dedicated to two people who have not only achieved success in building their own businesses around a niche but also wrote their own books, which in turn inspired me to write mine.

BRUCE BARTON, our work together informed much of the structure of this book. Without your introduction to your publishing contacts, I'm not sure this project would have ever made it off the ground.

MIKE ELLIOTT, you showed me that the concepts presented in this book can be applied to any business selling its expertise—including your wood canvas canoe restoration business.

Contents

Introduction

Finance had never been something I was interested in. In fact, the only D grade I ever received in school was in a finance class in college. Never would I have imagined that I would end up in a career in financial services.

But that's what happened. In 2005, during my last semester in graduate school, I was laid off from a marketing position. I had to figure out how to pay for school and my living expenses. I needed a job, and I needed it fast.

Throughout business school, I had been learning to be a marketing generalist. Most of my classes were focused on consumer product marketing and food service marketing. Case studies were focused on marketing behemoths such as Procter & Gamble and Starbucks. Marketing jobs in those types of corporations just didn't exist in San Diego. For the few marketing jobs in the area that did exist, there was a ton of competition, and I wasn't a very competitive candidate.

Through a referral from a networking contact, I fell into a job at a hybrid Registered Investment Advisor (RIA) that was heavily focused on marketing. The RIA I worked for was in high-growth mode. At the time, there were nearly forty employees, and the company was putting significant resources toward marketing.

While at the company, I organized public workshops at Sizzler. I coordinated a weekend radio show on an AM station. I placed ads in the *San Diego Business Journal*'s "Top Wealth Management Firms" awards issue. I coordinated client events. Basically, if there was a marketing activity that financial advisors were using in the mid-2000s, I did it!

Not only did I market financial planning and investment services, but the company also had a tax practice, an insurance division, and a sister estate planning law firm, all in the same building. Working there was a crash course in wealth management marketing.

A couple of years after falling into financial services, I found myself really enjoying it. The marketing was focused on two aspects I really enjoyed: relationship building and education. The services I was helping to promote actually made a real difference in people's lives. I realized that this was the industry where I wanted to spend my career.

Three years after first being hired at the RIA, I broke out to start my own financial services marketing agency. October 15, 2008, to be exact. Lehman Brothers had filed bankruptcy, the stock market was crashing, and the housing market was tanking. It was not a great time to be starting any business—especially not in financial services. But marketing financial advisors was all I knew how to do. And starting a business was a decision I had put in motion ten months earlier when I told my employer of my plans to start my own company. I couldn't pull out of the decision now just because the country was facing the worst financial crisis since the Great Depression.

In late October of 2008, I found myself with a brand-new business with only two clients during one of the worst periods in the financial services industry's history. My future was not looking bright. Then, it got worse. My only two clients ended up in a legal dispute over a few employees, and I found myself having to choose which one to work with. I was left with only one client and not making anywhere close to what I was previously making as a full-time employee.

I didn't have much money saved up. In fact, I only had a small amount of savings in my retirement accounts (that I couldn't access) and a $17,000 line of credit. Single and living alone, I had no one but myself to rely on financially. And I didn't have a viable Plan B. There was very little chance of me finding a full-time, salaried position in financial services marketing while the markets were in free fall. Uber didn't exist yet. My only option was to make my new business work before blowing through my line of credit. That, or— at the age of thirty—move back in with my mother, who lived five hundred miles away.

Desperate to make my business work, I did the only two things I could think of to do at the time: write and network. I attended any financial advisor networking event I could find just to meet people. And I wrote what I knew about financial services marketing in a blog and emailed it to the advisors I had met at the networking events. I realized I needed a bigger audience than just my email list, so I started posting my blog on LinkedIn groups and then on Twitter. From there, my business started to grow. I picked up clients locally in San Diego but also in Puerto Rico and Orlando. The articles I posted on social media started getting noticed, and popular industry publications asked me to write articles for them. Those articles led to speaking engagements. In just a couple of years, I had more than replaced the income I had earned as an employee, and I had a team of four employees.

From 2008 to 2020, my firm primarily helped fee-only RIAs develop and implement marketing plans. We have worked on every marketing collateral and campaign you can imagine—websites, brochures, workshops, radio shows, podcasts, videos, social media, client events, client referral strategies, center of influence referral strategies, search engine optimization, ads—and the list goes on. My company worked with firms just starting out to as large as $3 billion in assets under management (AUM). Our sweet spot was $100 million to $500 million in AUM.

During those twelve years, marketing was getting harder. While digital marketing made marketing more accessible to businesses of all sizes, it was also adding complexity and noise. To market a business today, it feels like you need to be an expert in search engine optimization, Google ads, social media, video marketing, webinars, podcasts, and marketing automation systems, just to name a few. And the rules of the game constantly change, which means you have to keep changing your strategy just to keep up. Even with a marketing agency employing specialists in different areas of marketing, I found it harder and harder to keep up.

Then COVID-19 happened. It completely disrupted the marketing landscape for financial advisors. Social distancing protocols and lockdowns made marketing through personal relationships, such as referrals, more difficult. In-person interactions, workshops, and client events were canceled. The traditional way advisors had marketed their businesses nearly came to a halt in the spring of 2020.

In response to the changing environment, many firms shifted to digital marketing channels such as social media, search engine optimization, and webinars. As a result, digital marketing channels became saturated, making it difficult for firms to get noticed, especially when going head-to-head against financial companies with larger marketing budgets and staff. It felt as if every financial advisor was now online, saying they worked with high-net-worth individuals and families.

Marketing, which was already challenging, got that much harder. But there was one group of advisors I worked with who didn't skip a beat. They were the ones who had clear expertise working within a niche. They had been focusing on creating awareness and credibility within their niche for years. Even prior to the pandemic, attracting clients to these firms didn't necessarily require in-person interactions. They had truly positioned themselves as different from other advisors and weren't competing in all the online noise. Their marketing strategy suffered very little disruption compared to the generalist firms I worked with during those initial months of the pandemic.

From my personal experience with my own business, I knew that marketing to a niche was easier than marketing to the general public. I knew generalist marketing required unnecessary hard work to stand out and get noticed. I knew there was an easier and more effective approach—niche marketing. I felt exhausted from hitting my head against the wall trying to come up with new ways to market the same old thing. In January 2021, I decided it was time for a change. I niched down and exclusively accepted new advisors as clients who also wanted to focus on a niche.

If you are frustrated with your marketing, I understand your frustration. And I know there is a better way. Through this book, I will show you this better way.

The recommendations in the book are not only from fifteen-plus years working with financial advisors and the insights from the advisors and experts I interviewed but also from my personal experience applying them to my own business.

Niche marketing has helped create success for both my firm and the advisors we work with. Whether you are a solo advisor or run an enterprise RIA, this book can help you. Although this book was written for the independent, boutique RIA, I believe all advisory firms can benefit from niching. The next section offers suggestions for adapting the strategies in this book depending on your firm type.

HOW TO USE THIS BOOK

When I first set out to write this book, I was writing it for the financial advisors I have primarily worked with throughout my career. These are owners of independent, boutique RIAs with AUM between $100 million and $500 million. When they come to me, they are struggling to get real traction in their marketing. Often these firms have one to three advisors and a handful of other employees, including associate advisors, client service associates, and administrative staff. These are the firms that've been in business for a while, building it by pounding the pavement to bring in clients. These RIAs have grown a respectable business through client referrals and personal relationships, but they've never been able to find a strategy that consistently brings in leads. The owners of these firms are motivated to find a better way to bring in clients than continuing to grind it out for the next couple of decades. While this book was written with this type of boutique RIA in mind, many of the strategies I discuss apply to all independent advisors and RIAs. (I will reference adaptations throughout the book.) If you don't fall into this boutique RIA category, here is how to adapt the advice to your own situation.

Solo Practitioners

Solo practitioners who are just starting their businesses are in a great position to begin with a niche. This could be the twenty-something advisor breaking away from their employer to create their own business or the thirty- or forty-something career changer starting an RIA from scratch. As you start, you should absolutely take any client who can pay your fees, but implementing a niche will focus your limited resources, so you are getting the most impact for your dollars and effort. While you need to make sure you have enough money to sustain the years it takes to build a niche practice, you will get much better results putting all your time, focus, energy, and money into one niche than if you spread yourself thin across multiple niches or have no focus at all.

The advisors I interviewed for this book, who started their businesses with very few financial resources behind them, niched almost immediately. With resources thin and no time to waste, the advisors I spoke with moved quickly to a niche. I did the same when starting my own business. In contrast, the advisors who had a longer runway, meaning more financial resources to sustain them when they started their business, initially chose a traditional generalist path and only later came to the conclusion they needed to niche when they weren't getting the results they wanted. While the sample size is small and the stories are anecdotal, this tendency to adopt a niche approach when you have no room for error suggests it is the more effective and efficient strategy for bringing in clients and revenue quickly.

Employee Advisors

If you are a "young" advisor employed by an RIA, you know you are at a disadvantage when it comes to attracting new clients to your firm. You most likely lack the network, relationships, and experience needed to convince prospective clients to work with you. And if you have chosen to work at an independent RIA, you probably don't possess the killer sales instinct that is stereotypical of financial advisors of the past. Instead, you may find yourself prioritizing servicing existing clients over marketing and business development.

Your employer likely hasn't equipped you with the marketing skills, knowledge, or resources you need. You may be expected to pound the pavement in the same way the owners did to build the business. But you know many of those tactics aren't as effective today, nor are they your natural marketing style. You need a different strategy than the traditional networking or cold-calling approaches of the past.

If you are young or new to the business, having a niche will help you overcome any perceived lack of experience (as measured by years). It will help you overcome the lack of a large network because you won't need long-standing personal or professional relationships to send you referrals. Word will spread about your expertise alone.

Whether you have ambitions to become an owner at your current firm or break off and start your own business, you'll need to be able to bring in clients. Rarely do pure "service advisors" ever end up with equity in a firm.

While you won't have the opportunity to implement all the areas mentioned in this book, you can choose a niche and focus your sales and marketing activities on it. If you start bringing in clients, you will be more valuable to the firm, incentivizing them to find ways to retain you. Or you will build up enough of a reputation that you can translate it to your own business someday. Even if you aren't allowed to take clients with you, you will have the marketing momentum behind you to set your business up for success.

Enterprise RIAs

While the ideal scenario is to focus the entire company on one niche, most $1 billion+ RIAs are too big for a course correction. Unless your firm started with a niche focus, it's unrealistic to assume it will ever transition to one niche for the entire firm. Instead, these firms should adopt a multi-niche approach. The company, as a whole, does not have a niche, but individual advisors are assigned to specialty areas—for example, business owners, women in transition, executives, and socially responsible investors.

Large RIAs with plenty of talent and deep pockets can easily pull this off. You should assign at least one financial advisor to spearhead each niche. And make sure you have the support staff and the financial resources to consistently implement multiple marketing plans at once.

Enterprise RIAs tend to gravitate toward general specialty areas (e.g., business owners, women in transition, executives) instead of the narrower niches I recommend in this book (e.g., family-owned businesses transitioning ownership to the next generation). Enterprise RIAs usually have a large client base and are trying to segment existing clients into one of the specialty areas and use it to mine more opportunities from this client segment. Because of the resources they can put behind their marketing, this strategy can be quite successful.

Can I Have More Than One Niche?

Before I show you how to implement a niche strategy into your practice, I want to answer one common question: Can I have more than one niche? If you are reading this from the perspective of an individual advisor, the answer is "no." If you are reading this from the perspective of your firm, the answer is "it depends."

Each niche requires its own marketing plan and its own champion to spearhead the effort. For example, let's say your niche is employees with equity compensation plans. You will need to have a website (or at least a webpage) for that niche. You will have to create content, such as blogs or videos, to demonstrate your expertise on topics directly relevant to your niche's financial pain points (no generic content!). You will have to optimize your website for search engines and implement strategies to drive people to your website. You will have to participate in online and offline communities where members of your niche gather. You will need to develop niche-specific campaigns (e.g., download an eBook, register for a webinar, attend an event). And you will need to have at least one staff member who takes full ownership of the niche to ensure this plan gets executed consistently.

Now imagine repeating this process for a second niche. Or multiple niches. Do you have the employee bandwidth to accomplish this? Do you have the financial resources to execute an entire marketing plan for each niche?

Unless you have both the staff and the financial resources to pull off multiple niches, you risk implementing two or more niche marketing plans poorly instead of implementing just one niche marketing plan well.

Having multiple niches can be tempting, but it can also dissipate your focus. Remember, the more niches you have, the more champions you need, and the more marketing plans you must implement.

Before you attempt two or more niches, review the rules of thumb we just discussed and ask yourself if you have the resources to go to battle on multiple fronts. If you don't, then concentrate your efforts on one niche. You will get better marketing results with less effort than if you attempt multiple niches. Plus, you can always pull the other niches off the back burner after you've succeeded with your current one.

WHERE TO START

This book is meant to be read as a whole or in parts. It starts from a ten-thousand-foot view and ends by really getting into the weeds. Here is what you can expect:

Part 1: An overview of the challenges financial advisors face when it comes to marketing and a prescription for how to remedy this.

Part 2: A framework to develop a niche marketing strategy in your business, including tactics to consider.

Part 3: A plan of action, including the exact tactics to use and when to use them.

While I think most readers will benefit from reading this book from cover to cover, if you are limited on time, you will want to pick the part that meets your interest. For those of you who are interested in high-level concepts and potentially new ways of thinking, I recommend Parts 1 and 2. For those of you who just want to know "how to get it done," read Parts 2 and 3.

If you are an employee advisor and are trying to get your boss to support your niche marketing strategy, have them read Part 1. If you are an owner and want to give direction to your team or outsourced partners, have them read Part 3.

A NOTE ON CASE STUDIES AND STRATEGIES

Throughout this book, I have included stories from financial advisors who are at various stages of working within a niche. Some started their niche just months prior to the interview, while others had been doing it for decades. I have included this wide range to show that niches can apply to all types of independent advisors.

While I was generous in including advisor stories, I purposely did not include too many specific marketing activities, tools, or trends in this book because they change so quickly and become outdated.

This book is designed to help you develop your high-level, long-term marketing approach (strategy) to achieve your business objectives. This strategy should stay the same for years—if not decades. The individual day-to-day actions (tactics) you utilize will change from year to year. This book will help you define your long-term strategy first, then you can apply whatever the latest marketing tactics are at that time, as long as they directly support your strategy.

But before you even begin to think about long-term strategy, much less day-to-day tactics, you need to know *why* you can't differentiate yourself with prospects. Knowing why the odds are stacked against you can help motivate the very necessary changes you need to succeed. In the first chapter, I describe why advisors cannot stand out from the competition and how becoming an uncomparable advisor is the remedy.

KEY TAKEAWAYS

- Solo practitioners just starting out are in an ideal position for a niche. Initially, they should not turn away any clients, niche or not, who can pay their fees. Meanwhile, they should put all their time, focus, energy, and money into building a successful niche marketing system.

- Young employee advisors can be at a disadvantage when it comes to attracting new clients. A niche can help them bring in clients, increasing their value to the firm or building a reputation that enables them to go out on their own.

- Enterprise RIAs may find it unrealistic to transition the firm to one niche. Instead, they can assign advisors to spearhead niches, using their support staff and financial resources to implement multiple marketing plans at once.

- Can you have more than one niche? For most firms and advisors, the answer is no. You probably do not have the staff, time, and money to go all in on multiple fronts. Even if you do, concentrate on one niche at a time.

- You may be chomping at the bit to implement marketing tactics, but you need to create a long-term strategy first. Only then should you select tactics, which you will pick solely because they support your strategy.

Part 1

THE BIG PICTURE

CHAPTER 1

All Financial Advisors Sound the Same

"You get personalized wealth planning and unmatched overall value." **—COMPANY A**

"We actually take the time to listen, to understand you and your goals so together we can find real-life answers to your real-life retirement." **—COMPANY B**

"We don't sell commission products. We are a fiduciary, obligated to act in our clients' best interests." **—COMPANY C**

Do these marketing messages sound familiar? Of course they do! Because they sound like every other financial advisory firm. I bet if I visited your website right now, you probably have similar language there.

The fact is that most financial advisors sound the same.

But there is one big difference between you and these companies. They have millions of dollars to spend on marketing to promote their message and you do not.

The quotes above were pulled directly from national television advertisements for Fidelity (company A), Charles Schwab (company B), and Fisher Investments (company C).

If your marketing sounds anything like the examples above, you are in trouble. You are no match against the strength of a national brand and multimillion-dollar marketing budget.

Right now, you are probably thinking to yourself, "I don't compete for clients with these companies. My prospects are looking for an independent advisor." That is probably true. And that makes it even harder to differentiate yourself. If your prospects were comparing you against a national brand name company, you could at least differentiate yourself by being independent, touting that clients are more than just a number, and explaining how the national brands don't really offer comprehensive financial planning. You would have some angle for being different.

The problem is that your prospects are probably evaluating other independent Registered Investment Advisors (RIAs), including roll-ups that can make the same claims you do. How can you make it clear to prospects that you are different from the other financial advisors they are considering?

Let's do a little exercise.

1. Write down how you would describe your firm to a prospect if they asked how you were different. To make this easier, you can take the first paragraph from your website.

2. Next, strip out all the words that most other RIAs also use or could use to make the same claim. For example, fee-only,

fiduciary, independent, comprehensive financial planning, transparent, best interest, retirement planning, CFP®,[1] full-service, commission-free, goals, etc.

3. Write down the words you have left that are not pronouns (e.g., *we*, *you*, *us*), prepositions (e.g., *from*, *to*, *on*), or articles (e.g., *a*, *an*, *the*).

As I'm writing this, I googled a random financial advisor website that had this message on the home page:

CUSTOM-TAILORED FINANCIAL PLANS

We work with you to make sure that you're always working toward your goals.

After stripping out all the words of this statement that every independent financial advisor could claim, I am left with nothing notable. In doing this exercise, you might not be left with any words that are meaningfully different to a client. I hate to break it to you, but that means you sound like every other financial advisor.

Here's the unfortunate truth. If you can't communicate a difference that is meaningful to prospects through your marketing, then they'll never get the opportunity to experience just how different it is to work with you. **If you offer real value and make a real difference in the lives of your clients, then you owe it to them to help make it easy to choose you.**

---

1 Certified Financial Planner Board of Standards Inc. owns the certification marks CFP®, CERTIFIED FINANCIAL PLANNER™, CFP® (with plaque design) and CFP® (with flame design) in the U.S., which it awards to individuals who successfully complete CFP Board's initial and ongoing certification requirements.

IT'S HARD TO SELL THE INVISIBLE

It's hard to sell an invisible, intangible service. Unlike with a physical product—where you can at least, in part, judge quality based on what you see and feel with your hands—prospects can't judge an advisor's quality by the clothes they are wearing, the furniture in their office, or their Zoom background.

When a prospect does try to evaluate various financial advisors, they find that most look and sound the same to them, making it difficult to choose the right one. From the prospect's perspective, most financial advisors offer the same basic services (e.g., financial planning, investment management, retirement planning), work with the same typical client (high net worth, probably nearing retirement), for the same similar fee (1 percent of AUM or so).

Most financial advisors also claim (accurately or inaccurately) that they are good at the most important services a prospective client is looking for—including comprehensive financial planning, retirement planning, and investment management—in the exact same way as every other advisor making the same claim.

Prospects Have Too Many Similar Choices

With an estimated 200,000 to 300,000 personal financial advisors in the United States, prospective clients have too many similar choices.[2] On top of that, unless prospects themselves are in a field that requires them to interact with a lot of financial advisors (for example, CPAs or attorneys), chances are that they probably have

---

2 Stephanie Horan, "States With the Most Financial Advisors Per Capita—2021 Study," Smart Asset, October 1, 2021, https://smartasset.com/data-studies/states-with-the-most-financial-advisors-per-capita-2021-study; Michael Kitces, "3 Reasons Why the Financial Advisor Market Size Isn't Actually Shrinking," Kitces.com, November 15, 2018, https://www.kitces.com/blog/financial-advisor-headcount-total-addressable-market-tam-technology-hiring-growth.

never evaluated more than one or two—if any—before. In other words, most prospects aren't qualified to evaluate which financial advisor is best. They simply have no experience with it.

And when prospects can't evaluate based on qualifications, they will resort to other factors to aid their decision-making. These factors can include the following:

1. **Pricing:** Prospects go for the lowest price.

2. **Personality:** Prospects happen to like one advisor more than another.

3. **Referral:** Prospects received a recommendation from someone they know.

4. **Marketing:** Prospects like one advisor's marketing the best.

5. **Credibility:** Prospects choose an established (probably national) brand they think is a "safe" choice.

I probably don't need to convince you how hard it can be to stand out as a financial advisor. It's something you've lived. It's something most advisors have lived.

And it can be a problem that drives you out of operating your own business, like Cathy Curtis (owner of a boutique RIA) almost experienced when starting her own business.

Cathy had a successful career in the food product industry, but she always felt a pull toward her passion—following the stock market, learning as much as she could about personal finance, and understanding how she could be more financially successful herself. Deep down, she had always felt she was destined to have her own business in finance.

"It took me a long time to make the leap," she said, "because I wanted to start my own firm and not go to work for another company. And I wanted to be financially stable first before doing that."

When Cathy reached the financial milestone she set for herself, she quit her career of twenty years and started her own financial planning and investment management business. As she explained, "One day, I was doing food product marketing. The next day, I was a financial planner."

Cathy quickly discovered, though, that starting a generalist financial planning practice that looked like so many other financial firms was no easy task.

"It was super rough going for the first five years. I got clients here and there. I lucked out in getting a wealthy client who ended up referring people to me, which helped. But five years in, I was nowhere near making the money that I needed to make. And that's when I started thinking that I had to do something different."

Cathy followed the path many advisors do when starting their own business. She had a canned website from one of the popular advisor website companies that use traditional stock photos and blue as an accent color.

"It looked like a website for a corporation, not for a woman running her own business. I thought, 'This isn't going to work. I'm going to have to decide what to do. I'm going to either get out of this or go to work for someone else . . . just do something else.'"

As much as she loved the industry, Cathy faced a marketing problem many advisors face when they all sound the same. Luckily, as you will learn later in this book, Cathy discovered the solution to her problem when she began to focus on self-made women in the Bay Area, and she developed her entire client experience around them. In the eyes of these women, Cathy became *the* advisor for them. She easily stood out, which is what this book's framework will help you do.

MARKETING DOESN'T HAVE TO BE HARD

Marketing is hard when you have a business that sells the invisible and where prospects can't tell the difference between you and the competition. This often results in a struggle to attract a consistent flow of ideal clients. You rely heavily on referrals from your network or existing clients for new growth.

Advisors in these situations often resort to brute-force marketing—relying on an enormous amount of effort and money to force themselves in front of prospects. They throw tons of money at marketing technologies and services, hoping one of them will be the silver bullet—only to discover they never work. Or they try to master the latest marketing trend to take advantage of it in the narrow window of time before it becomes widely adopted by other advisors. In the worst-case scenario, they give up on marketing altogether because they just don't think the return on their time and money is worth it. How to create a sustainable marketing system that consistently generates leads eludes them.

If this sounds like you, first, know that you are not alone. The reason you are struggling to consistently attract clients is not that you are implementing the wrong tactics (the individual marketing activities or actions). In fact, the tactics you are using might even work if used to support a clearly defined, long-term strategic approach.

The reason you are struggling to attract clients is that you are trying to get the attention of everyone, which results in getting the attention of no one. You are casting too wide of a net, trying to attract anyone who needs your services and will pay your fees—but you don't have the money or staff to reach such a large audience. You aren't large enough to pull off the brute-force marketing approach that companies like Fidelity, Charles Schwab, and Fisher Investments use.

Yet as difficult as marketing financial advisor services can be, it's also true that attracting clients who need your help doesn't have to be a struggle. There is a solution.

The solution is not to differentiate your firm in some minor way that prospects won't even notice. It's not to try to out-market your competition using the latest marketing trends or technology.

The answer is to change the playing field completely so that clients choose you based on your expertise. The answer is to become uncomparable—so different that comparison ceases, eliminating the competition altogether.

INCOMPARABLE OR UNCOMPARABLE —WHICH ARE YOU?

You are certainly familiar with the commonly used word *incomparable*. Google's English dictionary defines it as "without an equal in quality or extent; matchless."

But you are probably less familiar with the uncommonly used word *uncomparable*. Though your spell-check and most popular dictionaries may fail to recognize the word, Vocabulary.com defines it as "such that comparison is impossible; unsuitable for comparison or lacking features that can be compared."[3]

What's the difference exactly? As Grammarist.com explains: "Two or more things that can't be compared with each other are uncomparable. Something that is so good that it is beyond comparison is incomparable."[4]

---

3   "Uncomparable," vocabulary.com, accessed February 20, 2023, https://www.vocabulary.com/dictionary/uncomparable.

4   "Incomparable vs. Uncomparable," Grammarist, accessed February 20, 2023, https://grammarist.com/usage/incomparable-uncomparable/.

Why should that be important to you? Because that difference can make or break your marketing strategy.

This distinction is key as you think about the way you differentiate your business. **Are you incomparable (the "best" in a sea of advisors who all claim the same thing), or are you uncomparable (so different no one can compare themselves with you)?** It's a subtle but important difference.

I find most financial advisors think they are incomparable . . . the best of, or at least better than, their competition. When I ask how their firm is different, their answers usually sound something like, "We actually provide comprehensive financial planning" or "We get to know our clients personally." That sounds great, but the "we do it better" marketing approach has problems, such as the following:

1. **What does it actually mean to be better?** It's subjective and not something you can concretely define or measure. Do you offer better strategies? Do you offer better service? Better investment performance? Who is to judge? Not only can you not prove it, but you also can't even say it. Saying you are better is promissory and a violation of SEC and FINRA rules. In this industry, "better" is a fuzzy concept that is hard to define and prohibited from being claimed.

2. **How do you evaluate better?** A prospect can't determine that you are better before they choose you. Whether a prospective client decides to work with you or someone else, by choosing one advisor, they lose any point of comparison. They can never feel absolutely certain that they have picked the "best" advisor.

3. **How do you maintain better?** You can't maintain being better forever. Let's say you *are* better than other advisors, maybe even the best. What will it take for the competition

to surpass you? One additional service? One more meeting per year? Being the best becomes a neck-and-neck horse race. You are under the constant stress of needing to improve to stay ahead of the competition.

The movie *There's Something About Mary* demonstrates the exact problem with trying to be better. In one scene, Ted, played by Ben Stiller, picks up a hitchhiker, and they talk about the hitchhiker's business idea.

Hitchhiker: You heard of this thing, the 8-Minute Abs?

Ted: Yeah, sure, 8-Minute Abs. Yeah, the exercise video.

Hitchhiker: Yeah, this is going to blow that right out of the water. Listen to this: 7 . . . Minute . . . Abs.

Ted: Right. Yes. OK, all right. I see where you're going.

Hitchhiker: Think about it. You walk into a video store, you see 8-Minute Abs sittin' there, there's 7-Minute Abs right beside it. Which one are you gonna pick, man?

Ted: I would go for the 7.

Hitchhiker: Bingo, man, bingo. 7-Minute Abs. And we guarantee just as good a workout as the 8-minute folk.

Ted: You guarantee it? That's—how do you do that?

Hitchhiker: If you're not happy with the first 7 minutes, we're gonna send you the extra minute free. You see? That's it. That's our motto. That's where we're comin' from. That's from "A" to "B."

Ted: That's right. That's—that's good. That's good. Unless, of course, somebody comes up with 6-Minute Abs. Then you're in trouble, huh?[5]

When you are competing for the mantle of "better," even if you can somehow claim the hard-to-define title, you are essentially 7-Minute Abs just waiting for 6-Minute Abs to be introduced to the market. And when you position yourself as better, you have decided to play your competitors' game. You are saying, "We are just like them, only better (for now)."

The reality is, no small business can expect to be the best. The better way to stand out is to be different. When you position yourself as unique, prospects can't compare you to any other advisor. Instead, there are clear distinctions the prospect can easily notice between you and other firms. You claim leadership in your space because there is no one else to compare you to. You become uncomparable.

Striving to be incomparable keeps you in an endless race against the competition that you can never win. When you become uncomparable, you win because there's no one else to race against you.

So, how do you become uncomparable?

You begin by owning a niche. You become an expert in solving one problem for one type of client, and you build your business model to uniquely service the needs of those people. You focus on developing and promoting your in-depth expertise with a narrow set of clients. And as a result, prospects seek you out because you specialize in solving problems for people just like them. They seek you out because few other advisors, if any, are serving that niche in the way you do. They're not worried about whether you're "better" than

---

5 *There's Something About Mary*, directed by Bobby Farrelly and Peter Farrelly (1998; Los Angeles, CA: 20th Century Fox, 2005), DVD.

other advisors; they simply know you are the advisor who can help them. This confidence gives them comfort—as it gives you success.

Building your business in this way requires intention and work, but it doesn't have to be a mysterious or overly complex undertaking. You can get there by bringing your attention to six different areas of focus gathered together in what I call the Uncomparable Framework. In Chapter 2, we'll begin diving right in.

GETTING READY FOR YOUR JOURNEY

Before reading any further, take a moment to check in with yourself. How do you feel about the journey you have embarked on? Nervous about how your existing clients or team might react? Excited to finally stop the struggle to differentiate yourself? I imagine you have a mix of thoughts and emotions, and they are all valid. This book will cover how to manage your concerns while teaching you a framework to create a successful niche practice. I recommend you take stock once again at the end of your journey to savor how far you have come. You will no longer struggle to get the attention of prospective clients. Instead, they will come to you because you will be uncomparable.

KEY TAKEAWAYS

- All financial advisory firms look and sound the same to prospects. You are no match against the national brands and their multimillion-dollar budgets, and when you try to cast a wide net in your marketing, you cannot stand out from other independent RIAs, including roll-ups.

- You sell an invisible, intangible service. Between this and the fact that you cannot stand out from the competition, you likely struggle to attract a consistent flow of ideal clients. Your current tactics probably fail to create a sustainable marketing system that consistently generates leads.

- You do not have to struggle to attract clients. You can become uncomparable. This is different from being incomparable, which forces you to constantly prove you are "better" than the rest. As an uncomparable financial advisor, you cannot be compared with other advisors. Prospects see you are different and seek you out.

- You can begin becoming uncomparable by implementing The Uncomparable Framework.

CHAPTER 2

The Uncomparable Framework

N ow that you've seen why you should aim to be uncomparable, let's talk about how you get there. There are six components to the Uncomparable Framework. In this chapter, we'll explore how you can work with each one on your journey to becoming uncomparable.

These six areas of focus are

1. **Niche:** The narrow set of clients who all share one specific problem that you solve

2. **Position:** The simple message that communicates the problem you solve and the transformation prospective clients can anticipate

3. **Community:** The people that make up your niche, as well as the places and groups they congregate in and the media they consume

4. **Expertise:** The breadth of knowledge and experience you showcase to solve your niche's problem and lead them to transformation

5. **Network:** The process of connecting to and developing relationships with your niche

6. **Business model:** The services, process, experience, and pricing you specifically designed to solve your niche's problem

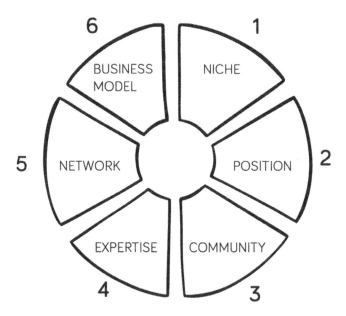

Some of these areas of focus within the Uncomparable Framework are, of course, part of any business strategy. Yet they look entirely different when approached with the intent to become uncomparable. To illustrate this, let's compare two examples using this framework—a generalist advisor and an uncomparable advisor focused on a niche.

GENERALIST ADVISOR

Company name: San Diego Financial Partners

Target client (not a niche in this case): Retirees and pre-retirees with $1 million+ AUM within thirty miles of our office

Position: We are a fee-only, fiduciary advisor helping individuals and families achieve financial peace of mind.

Community: San Diego County

Expertise: We demonstrate our knowledge of how we help clients achieve financial goals through purchased weekly market updates and other general financial planning articles.

Network: We keep in touch with the contacts on our email list by inviting them to monthly in-office "Lunch and Learns" on general financial topics such as social security, estate planning, and Medicare for clients and their guests.

Business model: We employ a team-based approach to implement comprehensive wealth management services following the seven-step financial planning process. We charge fees based on AUM.

UNCOMPARABLE ADVISOR

Company name: Aviation Capital Management

Niche: Commercial pilots who have irregular income streams

Position: We help commercial pilots stabilize inconsistent income from multiple jobs and self-employed gigs so that they can stop stressing about money and live more like a nine-to-five person.

Community: Airports, flight schools, and aviation organizations across the country

Expertise: We showcase our twenty years of experience serving pilots by writing original blog posts on the topics that are creating turbulence in a pilot's financial life.

Network: We keep in touch with the contacts on our email marketing list and social media accounts by inviting them to quarterly "Legends of Aviation" virtual fireside chats featuring famous pilots.

Business model: We offer guidance on the following: funding flight training, minimizing taxes as a 1099 contractor, choosing the right disability insurance, creating cash flow strategies for fluctuating income, and investing in the right retirement accounts. We charge an annual fee of $2,500, paid monthly, which includes managing up to your first $250,000 in investments. We then offer low-fee investment services beyond $250,000.

As you can see, the second advisor is clearly differentiated from the first in each of these areas. With uniqueness embedded into all six areas of the Uncomparable Framework, the second advisor has made it nearly impossible for another advisor to replicate their offerings and approach.

These six areas are aspects of any financial advisory business. In the Uncomparable Framework, we simply approach each with a new lens and intention that allows us to build something entirely different.

To be successful with a niche strategy, you don't have to work through the entire framework. In fact, I can't think of a single advisor I know that has completely reimagined all six areas. As you develop different components one at a time, you begin to become more differentiated from other advisors and start seeing progressive success along the way.

This framework will help you achieve success because it directs your time and attention. It guides you to know what people to network with, what centers of influence to meet, what events to attend, and what content to create.

By adopting the framework, you move away from being a generalist advisor trying to be "better" than every other generalist advisor. Instead, you use this framework to establish your niche, position, community, expertise, network, and business model so that you stand in a field of one. **Your marketing will become effortless over time as your ideal clients seek you out.**

A FRAMEWORK FOR MARKETERS AND NON-MARKETERS ALIKE

When I ask professionals who are considered experts in their niche what they do for marketing, a common answer is "nothing." They explain that others just know who they are and what they do, and people reach out to them. I attribute this non-marketing strategy to two things:

1. They focused on a niche early on in their business. They spent quite a bit of effort building out their reputation and a sustainable marketing infrastructure. Years or even decades after their initial investment, they are still benefiting by doing minimal "maintenance marketing."

2. They don't see what they do as marketing. They see it as sharing their knowledge and wisdom. They'll speak at a conference or be a guest on a podcast and not consider it

marketing—yet thought leadership can bring incredible sales and marketing benefits.

Does this kind of approach appeal to you? If so, good news—with this framework, in a few years, there's a good chance you will feel like you are doing "nothing" for marketing, too.

While advisors who love marketing will also thrive following this structure, this framework is tailor-made for financial advisors who don't like marketing. It's for the advisor who wants to build a good business while making a difference in the lives of their clients; who got into this business to help people, not to do public workshops; who rarely uses social media, thinking it's mostly a waste of time; who skips the marketing sessions at conferences; who ultimately doesn't want to do marketing but knows they have to.

If you don't love marketing, this framework is made for you. But that doesn't mean it will give you a quick and easy answer for your marketing challenges. **If a shortcut was possible, everyone would be doing it, and any competitive advantage would dissolve quickly.** What I'm recommending is hard, which means most people won't do it, giving you an advantage.

I like to use the flywheel metaphor when thinking about niche marketing. Small, consistent actions can build up momentum over time, leading to larger and more significant results. You have to put in real effort in the beginning, but once you achieve momentum, it takes much less effort to maintain. And you will see some quick successes along the way, which will motivate you to keep going.

I'm not going to recommend adopting the latest social media fad or tell you that you have to create certain types of content like videos. The purpose of this framework is to fundamentally change the way you think about marketing. **It will help you develop your big-picture**

strategy, and then you can fill in the individual marketing activities available to you that directly support that strategy.

This framework gives you permission to ignore marketing trends. You don't have to stress if the Google search algorithm changes or a social media site falls under new ownership. In other words, you won't have to become a marketing expert. But if you are a marketing expert, stick with me. When you implement the framework, you will see results even faster.

FROM THE BIG PICTURE TO THE DETAILS

This chapter has given you a big-picture view of the Uncomparable Framework, which can transform your business. Implementing it means you will no longer be a generalist vying with every other generalist. Instead, you will be a financial advisor no one else competes with. In the following chapters, we move from the macro picture to the micro as we cover each of the framework's six areas.

KEY TAKEAWAYS

- Marketing yourself as uncomparable follows a six-component framework. As you address each component (niche, position, community, expertise, network, and business model), you strengthen your uncomparable position.

- Niche marketing can lead to a low-maintenance marketing effort. However, this effortless approach requires hard work at the outset to launch the long-term strategy.

Part 2

THE FRAMEWORK

CHAPTER 3

Niche

So, you've decided to become uncomparable. The first step is to choose a niche, but what exactly is a niche?

A niche is a smaller segment of the larger market that has its own identity. Everyone shares similar characteristics and shares one unique problem. The problem a niche faces ideally requires a unique or complex financial planning strategy that most other advisors can't service profitably because they lack the business structure and knowledge to execute efficiently. This makes it something a focused advisor can, in time, master, deliver efficiently, and dominate.

Many advisors confuse a niche with a target market. They will say, "I have a LinkedIn campaign focused on the niche of executives." But that is just their target market for that specific campaign. A target market is the group of consumers that a company is trying to reach with its marketing efforts.

In the example above, the advisors haven't gained years of expertise working with that audience, they haven't designed their business to specifically serve that audience, and they still work with a variety of other clients at the same time. This is not a niche.

Specializing in a niche requires a deeper level of commitment to your ideal client. It means designing your business to serve the needs of this narrow segment. **Your niche dictates your brand, the message you communicate, the services you offer, the content you create, the processes you employ, the technology you offer, and the staff you hire.**

TYPES OF NICHES

When advisors hear the words *niche market*, they're often thinking about a few very specific types of people, like business owners, widows, or pre-retirees. This is unnecessarily limiting, though, because you can actually choose a niche market based on any of five different categories: career, event, specialty, mindset/values, or affinity.

Let's look at some examples in each of those categories.

Career

This category includes professions, employers or companies, and industries. Some examples that would fall into this category are

- Attorneys who feel trapped in their careers and want to quit

- Business owners who want to sell their business as tax efficiently as possible

- Military personnel who want to protect their family if anything happens to them

- Federal employees who don't understand the complexity of their government benefits

- Employees of the hottest new tech company that had a recent IPO and who don't know what to do with their stock options

Event

This category includes money-in-motion events, life transition events, or life stages that require financial guidance. Some examples include

- Inheriting appreciated real estate
- The death of a spouse
- Getting remarried and blending families

Specialty

This category is a specific service, product, or solution you offer to solve a specific problem. Examples include

- Special needs planning
- Exercising stock options
- Divorce financial planning

Mindset and Values

This category includes religion, life philosophies, or cultural mindsets. Examples include

- Christians who want to invest and gift money in a way that is aligned with their values

- Foreign-born citizens who need to plan not only for their finances but the finances of their family back in their home country

- Philanthropists who want to give in a way that is most tax efficient and gives them the most recognition

Affinity

This category describes common connections people share. These can be hobbies, interests, and lifestyles. For example

- Private pilots who want to find ways to write off their hobby of flying as a legitimate business expense

- RV snowbirds who face tax issues in multiple states

- Parents who started families in their forties or fifties and face retirement and paying for college at the same time

As you can see, there are many options to consider when choosing a niche market.

Some markets you may be considering may fall into more than one category. For example, maybe you are looking at women who are divorcing as a niche. This falls into the event category because divorce is a life transition and a money-in-motion event, and it can also fall into the specialty category with a focus on divorce financial planning.

The key to choosing a niche market is that members share a similar identity with similar characteristics *and* one central problem they need to solve.

Let's explore what this would look like using the affinity category of golfers. I would consider this a target market (not niche) because there isn't a specific need you are servicing. Yes, the group members share a similar identity and characteristics. But they don't have one central problem you are solving. Some may be retiring, some may be selling a business, and some may be young professionals thriving in their careers. Because you don't have one compelling message that will resonate with all of them, you are basically still a generalist who is all things to all people. You just happen to target your marketing efforts to the golf course instead of at the local Chamber of Commerce. Golfers as a group don't need an expert in their niche to solve their problems since there is not one problem golfers face.

For golfers to be a niche, you would want to narrow your focus on something much more specific, like newly professional golfers who are finally making enough prize and sponsorship money to cover their $100,000+ in tour expenses and want to plan their finances around their volatile income.

BRAINSTORM POTENTIAL NICHES

When I speak with advisors looking to hire my company to help them launch into a new niche, it's common for them to first rack their brains trying to come up with a unique niche. But often the answer is right in front of them. It's the one they already have the most experience with but have never formally defined, the one they already have dozens of clients in or are already a member of.

You don't need to look too deeply. (If you do, it's probably going to require more effort on your behalf to achieve success.) Picking a niche shouldn't feel like searching around wildly for a needle in a haystack. With a little bit of introspection, it should be fairly obvious. Most often, it should feel like you are uncovering and narrowing in on what is already there, like the experience Bruce Barton (owner of a boutique RIA) had in picking his niche.

Bruce Barton started his career in the tech industry, first as an engineer, then as a product manager, and later as an executive, working at several venture capital-backed startup companies.

"When it came time to think about joining my fourth tech startup," Bruce explained, "I found myself wanting to pursue a different entrepreneurial path. I decided to change careers in my late thirties to pursue my lifelong love of investing by starting my own RIA."

Like many advisors, Bruce built his business from the ground up, pounding the pavement to bring in clients. Since he was located in Silicon Valley and had previous connections in the tech industry, he naturally attracted tech employees, though, like most financial advisory firms, he also had the standard mix of other professionals like doctors, attorneys, and small business owners.

"For the first seventeen years of my business," he said, "I marketed to five very different and broad groups: people in tech, professionals, small business owners, divorcing spouses, and companies offering 401(k) plans. Then, at the advice of my marketing consultant, I decided to niche. Choosing my niche was obvious. I always enjoyed working with tech professionals and hearing the latest news in the industry. I especially enjoyed the startups because they reminded me of my early career. Working with tech was fun, knowing my work was valuable in helping the people who are such an important part of our economy."

Like Bruce, your niche will most likely be something you have experience with, either personally or professionally. You are just committing to specializing in that one thing.

To help the advisors I work with choose a niche, I developed a "Select a Niche" exercise to narrow down the possibilities of potential niche markets. You do this by exploring what lies in the intersection of your passion, your aptitude, and profitability.

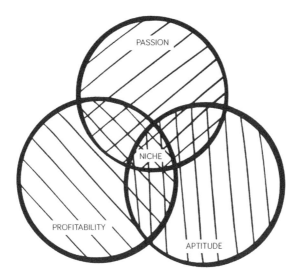

Passion

When brainstorming potential niches, start with the category of passion. If you can build your niche from here, you'll be doing something everyone hopes for but few achieve. And passion can be a strong driver that pushes you in the right direction. Beyond making your work more enjoyable and fulfilling, passion can bring healthy energy and excitement that is contagious—and can serve as a powerful motivator for prospects to choose you. To open up these possibilities, ask yourself

- What are my interests and passions?

- Who am I passionate about working with?

- What type of people do I naturally network with or spend time with?

- What would I be doing if I weren't a financial advisor?

- Which types of clients are enjoyable and easy to serve?

- Is there an area I have a strong interest in?

Aptitude

The next area to explore is your aptitude. Your aptitude comes from your natural talents, current and past professional experience, and even life experience. Ask yourself

- What types of clients do I have experience working with?

- What specializations do I have that my clients value most?

- What unique educational background do I have?

- What makes me an exceptional financial advisor?

- What is unique about my career and life experience?

- What hole in the industry do I naturally fill?

- What complex financial planning scenarios have I solved for clients?

- What personal strengths do I have?

Profitability

Finally, you need to look at profitability—because even if you have the passion and aptitude for serving a particular niche, you won't be successful if you can't make money. Ask yourself

- What types of clients have enough income (even if they don't have the assets) to pay for my minimum annual fee?

- What types of clients have enough investable assets to meet my minimum account size?

- What types of clients, if charged a percentage of net worth, would meet my minimum annual fee?

- What types of clients are most willing to pay my fees?

Note: If you work for a firm with a strict minimum account size and will not waive the minimum even in situations when the client will reach the minimum within a couple of years, you must take this into consideration when brainstorming this area.

Take the time to thoughtfully brainstorm, and at the end of this exercise, you will hopefully start to identify commonalities shared by all three of these categories. This is your short list of potential niches to explore further.

While you want your niche to ideally be a somewhat naturally aligned fit, that doesn't mean it will always be an immediate, clear choice. For Lindsey Swanson (a solo practitioner), choosing a niche was a process.

Lindsey knew she was looking for an underserved market, one that needed help but didn't fit the AUM model. She had relocated with her husband to rural Humboldt County, located five hours north of San Francisco, and this also presented specific opportunities.

If you haven't been, Humboldt County is primarily famous for two things: magnificent coastal redwood trees and cannabis. The county's legal cannabis industry is primarily run by entrepreneurial and anti-establishment men in their fifties.

"The cannabis industry seemed like a natural market for me," Lindsey said. "I had a few friends who were legal growers who offered to hire me as a consultant. They would never trust a traditional suit-and-tie financial advisor, but they trusted me, and I was only twenty-seven."

It takes a lot of work to establish a niche, and it requires a deep understanding of the business you serve. It's a commitment that should not be taken lightly. As Lindsey stepped into her clients' world, she was confronted with a number of challenges she never would have expected as a financial advisor.

"The women in their lives were either sugar babies or sex workers," Lindsey explained. "It took a lot of work to train the men to treat me as a professional and not as a paid female companion. There were also a lot of safety concerns about having to meet my clients at their place of business. A bodyguard was required. I thought to myself, 'Does it have to be this hard?'"

As Lindsey continued getting to know her clients better, she found it easier to relate to the girlfriends than the growers. "I began talking to a lot of the sex workers that were interacting with the cannabis community. Because we were around the same age, they trusted me. They loved how bubbly and positive I was."

Lindsey now found herself working with a few growers and a few sex workers and wasn't sure what direction she should go. That's where the Select a Niche worksheet came in.

"I scribbled down my skill set, who I related to and could be myself with, and who had money to pay my fees. Sex workers became the obvious answer. And even though I come from a conservative midwestern background, because many of the sex workers are younger women, we are of a similar generation and share similar humor and mindset. It's a very natural market for me."

Lindsey's niche took some time to determine with a few detours, but her unconventional path brought her to exactly what she was looking for and needed in her niche: an underserved market she could connect to (and, importantly, feel safe around).

Selecting a niche might be a process for you too. Give it the time and consideration it needs.

EVALUATE YOUR NICHE

I'm often asked, "Which niches are most successful?" There is no such thing as a perfect niche market. Only *you* can decide which option is right for you based on the characteristics of your target audience and your passion and aptitude to serve them.

While there is no guarantee that the niche you choose will be a success, you can reduce your risk by assessing the niche candidates you are considering on ten key factors that can impact your ability to launch a successful niche marketing strategy. These factors fall into two categories: the viability of the niche itself and the fit of the advisor.

Niche Viability

Does the niche itself present a viable opportunity?

- **Pain:** Is your niche feeling real pain regarding their problem?

- **Urgency:** Is it urgent for your niche to have their problem solved?

- **Complexity:** Is the primary financial problem for this niche something that takes a lot of time and research to solve for the first client but would be easy to replicate once you have developed the expertise and a process?

- **Purchasing power:** Is your niche willing and able to pay your fees?

- **Growing:** Is your niche market growing?

- **Easy to target:** Is your niche easy to find for marketing purposes (e.g., purchase lists, associations, groups, social media targeting)?

- **Dominance:** Is your niche narrow enough to dominate this space due to a lack of competition in this specialty?

Advisor Fit

How well-suited is the advisor for this niche?

- **Expertise:** Do you have the basic skills and knowledge necessary to begin serving this niche?

- **Credibility:** Do you have a minimum amount of credibility working with clients in this niche (e.g., at least one client is, or you are, a member of the niche)?

- **Access:** Can you access the niche through your existing network and opportunities?

Let's look at each of these a little deeper.

Pain

Is your niche feeling significant mental or emotional pain regarding their problem? The more pain a prospect feels about their specific financial problem, the more likely they will act to solve it.

For example, someone who receives a sudden windfall, such as the sale of property or the exercise of stock, faces the very real pain of taxes. Someone who is suddenly single after a divorce or death of a spouse and managing their personal finances for the first time faces the pain of not knowing if they can survive on the money they have.

In contrast, someone who is retiring in fifteen years with a guaranteed pension may have a nagging concern they aren't doing everything they could about their finances, but they are experiencing the same level of pain as widows/widowers or recipients of sudden windfalls.

When Marlon Wesh (a solo practitioner) was choosing a niche, he centered around this key factor. He pursued a niche he had no experience with but knew was underserved with significant financial pain.

"For most people, financial planning is a luxury," he said. "It's a nice-to-have, not a must-have. When I started my business, I had a one-year-old, my wife and I had just bought a house, and we were living off her salary as a speech therapist. I didn't have time to try to sell a nice-to-have service. So, I started thinking, 'What is it that people cannot get away from? Something that is not nice to have, but is a must-have?'"

The answer was clear . . . taxes! Marlon began looking for people who had complicated tax issues. Business owners were an obvious choice, but Marlon didn't feel that would be a good fit for him. Then, through an internet search, he stumbled upon traveling nurses. Since traveling nurses may have to pay state income tax in whichever states they work, after working in four or five states in one year, they end up with a complicated tax situation. This was a niche that had complex financial issues and a "must be solved" tax issue.

Picking a niche that has a clear pain point, as Marlon did, will make your marketing easier and your service more in demand.

Urgency

Is it urgent for your niche to have their problem solved? The more urgent it is for your niche to solve their problem, the easier it is for you to attract them.

For example, dealing with the immediate aftermath of a spouse's death is an urgent need. Someone who has money scattered across different employers and investment accounts and just wants to get their finances organized doesn't feel the same sense of urgency to solve their problem.

If there is no urgency, don't automatically eliminate the niche. But be prepared for a longer, more difficult sales and marketing process.

Complexity

Is the niche's primary financial problem complex enough that most other financial advisors can't address it adequately or profitably? Complexity is one of the key factors that will help protect your dominance in a niche.

If your niche has an issue that takes a lot of time and research, most advisors will not adequately serve these clients. But once you have worked with several of these clients and developed the expertise and a process, you can profitably serve these clients in a way the competition can't.

Jane Mepham (a solo practitioner) works in a niche that faces layers upon layers of complexity, helping foreign-born American permanent residents, citizens, and those on work visas with their cross-border financial issues.

She explains: "First, there is the technical knowledge that is required in understanding cross-border financial planning issues like visa status and tax treaties. Then, there is cultural understanding. I worked with a client who was on an immigrant visa, and he told me he has to support his five siblings back in his home country. He needed me to come up with a plan to make this work. I think most advisors would just tell him he needed to not send money back home, but that just wasn't an option."

As a woman who came to the US on a work visa to work in the tech industry, Jane is uniquely qualified to help her complex niche. The questions they have are the same questions she struggled with about her own finances before changing careers and becoming a financial advisor. Even currently, her niche may be too complex. During our interview, she admitted that the cultural differences from country to country made her niche challenging and that she is considering narrowing it down to specific countries in the future.

Purchasing Power

Is your niche willing and able to pay your fees? This is a must because if your niche doesn't have the means to pay your fees, you simply don't have a business. You deserve to get paid what your expertise is worth, and if your niche can't pay you, it's not a good choice. An ability to pay, though, does not necessarily need to mean they must have a minimum number of assets. You may have to find a creative pricing structure that matches your niche's financial situation (e.g., subscription, flat fee, or hourly).

While most financial advisors focus on the people who have enough assets to pay 1 percent AUM fees to be profitable, there is a world of opportunity with people who are underserved and yet still have the ability to pay for advice.

Lindsey Swanson describes the typical sex worker client who reaches out to her for her services. "I have a bunch of clients who come to me that are nineteen or twenty and will say, 'I just got my own place. I started on OnlyFans and it blew up, and I'm making forty thousand dollars or fifty thousand dollars every month. That's cool, but I have no idea what I'm doing with my money. My parents don't know what I do for a living, so I can't go to them for advice.' Most young women can ask, 'Hey, dad, what type of car insurance do I get?' Or, 'Mom, how do I apply to get a credit card?' But given the nontraditional work my clients do, they don't always have that family support. That's where I step in and add my value. I'm the safe person in their life where they can ask their financial questions and get advice that is actually in their best interest."

Your chosen niche will absolutely need a certain level of purchasing power for your business to succeed. Just remember, this could come in different forms, and it's worth exploring all the possibilities.

Growing

Is your niche market growing? While you don't have to pick a niche in a fast-growing market to succeed, you don't want to invest your time and money in a slowly dying market either.

For example, I have worked with a boutique RIA specializing in a utility company pension plan that was eventually phased out. While some employees got grandfathered in, new employees did not. It was clear this niche was no longer a long-term feasible client base. The firm needed to (and did) shift its business away from this niche.

Easy to Target

Is your niche easy to find for marketing purposes? Some niches will be easy to market to, and others will not. For example, finding a list of employees working for one business (e.g., Pfizer) is easy because you can search LinkedIn. Finding philanthropists is harder.

Can you easily find or purchase a marketing list of people in your niche (e.g., LinkedIn or a direct mailing list)? Can you easily identify where members of your niche gather together (e.g., conferences, associations, or Facebook groups)? Answering yes to these questions is a good sign that you'll easily reach your niche.

If you can't buy a list of prospects or determine where they gather, it doesn't mean that your niche is a bad choice. But it does mean you should be prepared for marketing to be harder for this niche.

In choosing his niche of traveling nurses, Marlon Wesh knew he wanted a group that was easy to target. That's largely because he first experimented with working with philanthropists and then first-generation professionals, the children of immigrants. "I realized these people were hard to pinpoint," he said. "Because it was so difficult to find these people, I started looking at other niche options."

When Marlon came across traveling nurses as a potential niche, he looked to see if there was a community that already existed for them to support each other around some common challenges.

"Lo and behold, there was. I found a fifty-thousand-plus Facebook group of traveling nurses." That's when Marlon knew he was on to something.

Dominance

Is it possible for you to dominate this space due to a lack of competition? How much other competition is there in your niche? Do you need to narrow the definition of your niche down further to dominate your specialty?

Let's look at an example of financial advisors serving business owners. While the general group may share a central problem—needing to eventually sell their business to fund their retirement—there is already a lot of competition for them. This means if you choose business owners as your niche, you will probably want to be even more specialized so you can dominate the space. In this instance, you may narrow your niche to work with individual partners within a business who want to sell their stake. Sure, your competition may deal with clients like these, too, but you can become the dominant expert if that's all you do.

Expertise

Do you have the skills and knowledge to serve this niche? When you are just starting with a niche, you probably won't have a lot of true expertise just yet, but you should have some basic skills to serve this group.

For example, when I started my business in 2008, I had previously held a marketing position within an RIA for three years. While I definitely was not the expert in my niche that I am today, I had the basic skills and knowledge to help my first few clients.

You will develop increasing expertise as you work with niche clients, and in the meantime, you can further enrich your understanding by studying your niche as much as you can.

Credibility

Do you have credibility working with clients in this niche? If you have zero experience with your chosen niche, it will be hard to convince the first few clients to work with you.

For example, I once spoke with an advisor who thought airline pilots would be a good niche. But he had never worked in the airlines and didn't have any airline clients. He had no established credibility, which would make that niche very difficult for him.

If you don't have professional experience working with a niche, do you have personal experience? Or perhaps you are in the niche yourself. For example, if your niche is families with special needs children, it's okay if you don't have any clients in this niche if you yourself have a child with special needs. You would have immediate credibility with this niche because you are part of it.

Access

Do you have an existing network or other opportunities to reach your niche? How much access you have to your niche will make all the difference in your ability to market.

Say you want to work with physicians at Kaiser Permanente. While they are easy to target in that you can find a list with contact information on the Kaiser website, this is not an easy group to get in front of. But if your spouse is a Kaiser physician, they can help you gain access to that network.

The best-case scenario is if you are a member of the niche (e.g., your niche is special needs planning, and you have a child with special needs). Even if you don't currently have access to your niche, you can gain access by joining organizations on online forums of people just like you. But if you aren't a member of the niche, you will want to make sure you have other ways to access the group.

While there are exceptions, like Marlon Wesh and his traveling nurse niche, it will generally be more difficult to pursue a niche if you don't have some sort of "in" or experience with it.

Your Niche Evaluation

Use these ten factors to determine whether you have a viable niche. Although you do not need to be strong in all ten, the more areas you feel confident in, the less likely your niche will be a bust. That being said, in my experience, the strongest niches will have purchasing power, are easy to target, and have complex financial needs, and you need to have a high degree of access to it either through being a member yourself or through a conduit like a center of influence (COI).

IS YOUR NICHE LARGE ENOUGH?

A common question I get is whether a niche is large enough. It depends on your growth goals and how many clients you want. Do you want ten clients, one hundred clients, or one thousand clients?

In my experience, advisors are more likely to pick a niche that is too broad. Never have I seen an advisor choose a niche that is too small. I never worry that a niche is too narrow because the advisor can always expand it (i.e., niche up). You may even find that your niche naturally broadens as you dominate your market.

Let's say your niche is employees working at a specific athletic shoe company in the Pacific Northwest. While your marketing focuses on employees of that one company, you also live in the athletic apparel capital of the United States. Your clients often switch from one company in the industry to another. As your clients change jobs, you inevitably learn the ins and outs of the equity compensation and benefits of these other companies. And because your clients love the work you do for them, they refer colleagues at their new companies to you.

While you started a niche at the company level (one specific shoe company), you end up with a niche at the industry level (athletic apparel). The expansion is natural.

The important thing is to pick a niche and focus your marketing efforts on that one niche. Time and experience will tell you whether your niche is too small. By then, you will have new knowledge to guide you on which direction to expand.

A LOCAL OR NATIONAL NICHE: WHICH IS RIGHT FOR YOU?

You may be wondering if you should focus your niche on your local area or expand to a national level. There are several factors that should be considered when making this decision.

1. Are there enough people in your niche locally?

    a. **If yes, stay local.** If you are in a densely populated area with tens of thousands of people in your niche (e.g., tech workers in Silicon Valley), the pool of potential prospects is large enough that you should focus your initial efforts locally and expand only when you run low on opportunities.

    b. **If no, go national.** If you are in a geographically remote location, you will need to consider a national niche because it is unlikely there are enough potential clients in your area to sustain your business.

2. How broad is your niche?

    a. **If broad, stay local.** If you have a broad niche, such as one involving widows, business owners, or divorcees, focus your efforts on your local market. There is quite a bit of competition in these broad niches in every geographic market, so you need to narrow the pool of potential clients as much as possible for word-of-mouth marketing to spread.

    b. **If narrow, go national.** If you have a narrow niche and a rare specialty (e.g., owners of family-owned ranches and farms), go national. People will seek you out for your expert advice no matter where you are located.

3. Do large populations of your niche congregate in specific geographic areas outside of your local area?

    a. **If yes, go national.** For example, if your niche is employees of a specific company that has major branch locations in several cities, you would consider a national niche or at least a multi-region niche.

b. **If no, stay local.** If there is no obvious reason to expand to specific geographic reasons, shrink your pool of prospects to the local community.

4. Does your niche relocate often?

a. **If yes, go national.** If you work with clients who live a location-independent lifestyle, such as traveling nurses, pilots, flight attendants, or digital nomads, you will end up with a national (or even global) niche whether you plan to or not.

b. **If no, stay local.** If your niche stays in one place, it's always best if you can be in the same geographic area for some good old-fashioned, in-person, face-to-face time.

Even if you ultimately plan to focus on a national niche, start locally if possible. It will be easier to network with and meet people face-to-face. Word-of-mouth marketing about your business will spread more quickly in a smaller pool of people. Then, once you get traction locally, you can expand your efforts nationally.

Just because you plan for a local niche doesn't mean you won't end up with a national niche. For example, if you primarily implement online marketing strategies that know no borders, a national expansion is likely to happen organically.

OVERCOMING YOUR FEARS

One of the biggest barriers to becoming uncomparable is overcoming the fear surrounding focusing on a single niche. Shifting to a single niche strategy is scary. I know this firsthand because I have niched twice in my own business. The first time was in 2008, when

I started a marketing agency exclusively serving independent financial advisors. The second time was in January 2021, when I decided to get more specific—niche down—to only work with RIAs who wanted to niche. So yes, I know, niching is scary! But let me help put some of your fears to rest.

Fear: Choosing a niche will alienate my existing clients. You don't have to change the way you currently do business right from the start. You can focus on a niche in ways that protect your existing client relationships. For example, you don't have to change your entire website. Instead, you can develop one page on your site dedicated to the niche. Your existing clients won't even notice that you've made this shift until you tell them.

Fear: If I niche, I'll have to turn away business. In the short term, you don't have to turn away business, and you can continue to work with whomever you like. You'll still get referrals who won't fit your niche, and you can decide if you say yes or no to working with them. Over the long run, when you become wildly successful at implementing the Uncomparable Framework, servicing non-niche clients will complicate your operations. To be uncomparable to your clients, you will design your process and services to meet their unique needs. Non-niche clients will be more difficult to accommodate and less profitable to service. Plus, you'll find you just don't want to serve them anymore because it is harder work.

Fear: Future advisors I recruit won't want to work with my niche. Having a niche can actually help attract the right talent to your firm, and an advisor who is drawn to what you are doing is likely to be a good cultural fit and service your clients well. You won't appeal to as many candidates, but you will be very attractive to the right type of candidate. This will possibly even give you an edge over other firms the candidates are considering.

Fear: I don't have enough experience to work with this niche.

Even if you have experience helping only one or two clients in your niche with their finances (including yourself if you are a member of the niche), you probably have more knowledge than your client about their situation. In the short term, you should learn as much about your niche as is publicly available. Each additional client you work with will increase your expertise. After working with a handful of clients, you'll start to feel more confident in your knowledge. After a year or two, you'll get over your imposter syndrome and start to feel like the legitimate expert you'll have become.

Fear: What happens if my niche dries up? It is rare that a niche will dry up completely, but it can have periods of booms and busts. Bruce Barton, the financial advisor niching in Silicon Valley tech professionals, explains: "The tech industry can be volatile. You go through periods when the industry is booming and then when it goes bust. You worry about generating leads when the landscape changes."

These shifts provide new opportunities. In Bruce's case, his firm adapts its marketing tactics to reflect the current environment. For example, during boom times, Bruce addresses the questions his niche has about managing their equity compensation ahead of liquidity events, such as an initial public offering (IPO) or acquisition. During a bust, he addresses the fears they have, from the amount of money lost to deciding whether it's time to move on to a new career opportunity. Because he has a niche, his message is better able to find the pain point and encourage action than a generic marketing message would.

If your niche is eliminated altogether, this still provides new opportunities. For example, if one company goes out of business, all of those employees will disperse to other companies, most likely in the same industry. This gives you an opportunity to expand to an industry-wide niche serving employees at those companies.

If a change to your niche does not present any new opportunities, you can switch to an entirely different niche. Once you have applied the Uncomparable Framework once, it is something you will know how to repeat in the future.

While it is common to be resistant to focusing on a niche, just know you don't have to change the way you do business from the start while you are building your new niche. You can make the decision about whether you want to change your business later, once your niche is so effective and profitable that it doesn't make sense to continue your current course any longer.

All that is required is that you dedicate all future marketing time, money, and energy to your niche. When the niche becomes wildly successful and you only want to work with that market (which you will!), you can address a legacy client transition plan at that time. But for now, it's not something you or your partners have to think about.

Your niche is a carefully considered and executed experiment. It is not uncommon for people to start down the path of one niche, which leads them to another niche. For example, I have worked with an advisor whose focus on divorcees led her down the path to working with divorce attorneys since that was whom she was networking with to reach her initial niche. Or you may start with a broader niche and niche down to a narrower specialization, such as going from working with business owners to working with owners of manufacturing businesses.

THE BENEFITS OF NICHING

While you can't be fully certain your initial niche will be successful, the niche strategy overall is extremely likely to yield positive results. When you choose a niche, you have a focus for all your marketing efforts. You no longer need to worry about whether this or that tactic will work. You simply ask yourself if your niche will resonate with it. You avoid frustration and dead-end strategies. What's more, you find your career even more fulfilling. You have combined your passion and talents into a profitable enterprise that makes a significant impact on the lives of the people you serve. And you'll also reap financial benefits, as a 2020 Kitces.com study shows. In the study, top advisors with a niche versus top advisors without a niche:

- Spend 150+ more hours every year on high-value, client-facing activities (or 28 percent more time with clients and prospects while spending 13 percent less time doing middle-office and back-office tasks)

- Are able to deliver a more focused and customized financial planning process (as not every possible area of financial planning is applicable to every particular niche)

- Serve an average of 14 percent more clients (since advisors with niches can more easily scale their practices)

- Have clients with an average of both 25 percent more investable assets and higher net worth

---

- Are able to set their AUM fees 9 percent higher and generate 20 percent higher standalone planning fees

- Earn an average of $660,000 (versus $395,000 for non-niche advisors at the same income percentile)[6]

Now, with a niche in hand, you will learn how to position yourself with your new prospective clients in Chapter 4.

KEY TAKEAWAYS

- You should choose a niche where everyone shares similar characteristics and faces a common problem. Solving the problem should require unique or complex financial planning strategies that other advisors do not offer.

- A niche generally falls into at least one of the following five categories: career, event, specialty, mindset/values, and affinity.

- When selecting a niche, use the Select a Niche exercise to understand the intersection of passion, aptitude, and talents.

- Assess the likelihood of success with your niche based on ten factors including pain, urgency, complexity, purchasing power, growing, easy to target, dominance, expertise, credibility, and access.

---

6 Derek Tharp, "Kitces Research on Advantages of Niching in Time Use, Planning Approach, Pricing, and Productivity," Kitces.com, August 24, 2020, https://www.kitces.com/blog/kitces-research-financial-advisor-niche-productivity-revenue-time-use-efficiency-pricing-models.

- Take some time to consider any fears you may have. Then respond to them clearly. Remember, you don't have to change the way you do business or turn away clients until you decide it is time.

TOOLS

Select a Niche Course

- For guidance on how to brainstorm your niche, visit OnNiche.com/select-a-niche to take the Select a Niche course.

Niche Assessment

- While there is no exact calculation to tell you whether a niche will succeed, the likelihood of success increases with the more affirmative responses you have. Visit OnNiche.com/assessment to take the niche assessment.

CHAPTER 4

Position

As we've discussed, most financial advisors look and sound the same to a prospect. In their eyes, most offer the same basic services, such as financial planning, investment management, and retirement planning. Most work with the same typical client: high-net-worth pre-retirees. And most all charge a similar price of around 1 percent of AUM plus or minus, depending on the portfolio size.

If you niche, though, you will no longer be part of this generic group. So how do you communicate a message that reflects that? How do you communicate a message that clearly differentiates you from the competition, making it easier for prospects to know you are the right advisor for them?

Once you've taken the first step—deciding to specialize in a niche—the next step in the framework is to develop a marketing message that communicates you as uncomparable. It should be simple, clear, and easy for everyone coming into contact with you to remember.

The best marketers in the world repeat one simple message over and over again. Geico has promoted the message that "15 minutes could save you 15% or more on car insurance" for decades. Its simplicity and repetition make the message memorable.

Simplicity, though, can be incredibly challenging.

Financial advisors often struggle with messaging because they get bored with their message and want to change it. Or they want to address all the different ways they can help a client because what they do is not simple. But even though what you do is not simple, it is your job to communicate it simply so people can understand.

In 1998, Steve Jobs shared his mantra of focus and simplicity with *BusinessWeek*: "Simple can be harder than complex: you have to work hard to get your thinking clean to make it simple. But it's worth it in the end because once you get there, you can move mountains."[7]

Marlon Wesh started his RIA just three years prior to our interview and only started working with his niche of traveling nurses eighteen months prior. During our interview, he told me the secret to his success was messaging.

"People think marketing is hard, but in reality, it is much simpler than they think. It's messaging. It's messaging, messaging, messaging. Traveling nurses come to me for two issues—taxes and making work optional. I only talk about those issues in everything I do."

When it comes to communicating a marketing message that people remember, clear and simple always win.

---

7 "Steve Jobs: 'There's Sanity Returning,'" *Bloomberg Businessweek*, May 24, 1998, https://www.bloomberg.com/news/articles/1998-05-25/ steve-jobs-theres-sanity-returning.

THE MESSAGING FORMULA

Developing a clear, easy-to-remember message can be constructed using the following formula:

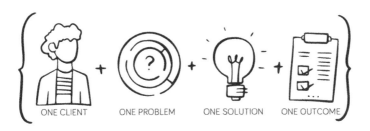

As an example, let's use the fictional uncomparable firm I mentioned in Chapter 2, Aviation Capital Management. Here is what their messaging formula would look like:

- **One client:** Commercial pilots

- **One problem:** Inconsistent income from multiple jobs and self-employed gigs makes budgeting for both today and the future almost impossible

- **One solution:** We have a system to help pilots stabilize their income

- **One outcome:** Live like a nine-to-five person knowing how much you can spend and save each month

With this formula, your simple message is:

For commercial pilots, inconsistent income from having multiple gigs is stressful. At Aviation Capital Management, our system helps pilots stabilize their monthly income so that they live more like a nine-to-five person.

That's it! All marketing messages going forward are some variation of this same message.

For example, Jackie Esperanza is the fictional owner of Aviation Capital Management, and she is hanging out at the local pilot's bar. While she's there, one of the pilots asks what she does for a living. She responds, "You know how commercial pilots are stressed out because they never know how much money they have each month? Well, we help them stabilize their income so they can live more like a nine-to-five worker."

The banner image on the company's website would say:

STABILIZE INCONSISTENT INCOME

FINANCIAL PLANNING FOR COMMERCIAL PILOTS

And the company description on Jackie's LinkedIn profile would read, "For commercial pilots, inconsistent income from having multiple jobs is stressful. At Aviation Capital Management, our system helps pilots stabilize their monthly income so that they live more like a nine-to-five person."

Of course, when working one-on-one with clients, Jackie would address the other common problems commercial pilots face, such as

- Lack of access to retirement plan accounts by employers

- Being underinsured from both a liability and disability standpoint

- Dealing with self-employment income issues

But if Jackie tried to communicate these other messages every time she told someone what she did, prospects and centers of influence would forget what she does. It's too much information to retain for someone not intimately involved in her business.

In his training, Donald Miller, author of the bestselling book *Building a StoryBrand*, describes it this way: "Every time you hand someone a piece of information, you are handing them an eight-pound bowling ball. And if you hand them too much information, it's literally like handing them too many bowling balls. They will drop them all."[8]

Instead of trying to communicate all this information in marketing materials, Jackie would hand out these additional bowling balls of information on other topics in her content marketing (e.g., blogs, videos, podcasts, eBooks, webinars, and presentations). But even then she would make sure she always brought her content back to the core message of "stabilizing your income to live like a nine-to-five worker."

For example, she would develop a presentation for aviation organizations on the five steps commercial pilots need to take to stabilize their income. She would include details such as "dealing with both self-employment income" as one of the steps to stop their feast-or-famine lifestyle and instead live like a nine-to-five person.

Let's break this formula down further.

ONE CLIENT

In Chapter 3, you chose a specific niche you are going to serve. Now it's time to drill down to one specific client within that niche. To do

---

8 Donald Miller, "Avoid Giving Too Much Information | Donald Miller clip," FranklinCovey, July 26, 2019, video, https://youtu.be/mG1RnKopQHY.

this, you are going to create a fictional representation of your ideal client, which is referred to as an avatar or a persona.

A persona contains important details about your ideal niche client, such as demographics, psychographics, financial profile, and backstory. It directs your messaging, branding, content, and campaigns, and it keeps your marketing focused. It is not something you will ever show to anyone outside of the company. **Once you have developed your persona, every marketing decision going forward should be answered through the lens of "Would this resonate with my persona?"** If the answer is "no," then it's back to the drawing board.

When ideal niche prospects go to your website, consume your content, or scan your list of services, you want them to feel that your business was created just for them. Personas help create that experience.

When creating personas, my advice to you is to start simple. Start out by answering questions like: What is their name, age, and family status? What is their annual household income? How much do they have in investable assets? Once you have some of the basic details, you can slowly start to fill in more specific pieces of their story, such as their careers, financial concerns, and financial ambitions.

To make this easier, I suggest that you think of an existing client who matches your ideal client profile and tell a modified version of their story. Or you can combine the story of a few clients into one. Let's take a look at the fictional Aviation Capital Management's example persona.

CHELSEA, COMMERCIAL PILOT

Age: 35

Employment: Commercial pilot

Family Status: Single

Homeownership: Rents an apartment

Annual Household Income: $175,000

Net Worth: $50,000

Investable Assets: $100,000

Scenario: Chelsea is under a lot of stress. She works as a pilot for a couple of private jet charter carriers, and she has a side hustle as a flight instructor to supplement her income. While Chelsea makes a good living, her income can fluctuate drastically from month to month. She never knows how much she can afford to spend or save, and she finds herself saying "no" to activities with family and friends because she's not sure if she'll need the money next month. Chelsea is tired of the feast-or-famine lifestyle and wants to have the same income security that her nine-to-five salaried friends enjoy.

Chelsea has decided to seek out a financial advisor who can help her feel financially stable. She wants an advisor who will put the systems in place that allow her to live off the same amount of money each month, no matter how much or little she worked. Now that she is making good money, she'd like to pay off her flight school loans, build her savings, and make sure she's putting the right amount of money in the right accounts for her eventual retirement. And most of all, she'd like to quit worrying about how much she can spend each month and start enjoying the good income her livelihood provides.

Primary Financial Challenges:

1. Smoothing out inconsistent and unreliable income

2. Having a set budget each month so she feels free to spend money, enjoy life, and achieve financial goals

3. Understanding the best retirement saving vehicles for her situation and how much she can afford to contribute each month

4. Paying off the debt she incurred during flight training

When creating your own persona, here are the basic things to start with:

- Choose a gender, age, nationality, and name. (Make sure the name is age-appropriate, matches your geographic area, and reflects the nationality of your persona.)

- Pick a memorable title to easily identify your persona (for example, Chelsea, Commercial Pilot).

- Pick a photo from Google images or a stock image website like iStock that aligns with your persona and looks like an authentic picture of someone who would be your client. The picture should also provide context around the persona's lifestyle. For example, for a commercial pilot, there would be a plane in the background. (Note: Be sure to obtain the proper license to use the image in your marketing materials.)

- Determine other basic details like their family status, their annual household income, and how much they have in investable assets.

From here, you can start to further explore their financial and life situation. To help you do this, answer these questions:

- What event is triggering them to evaluate their finances?

- What are their concerns and worries?

- What are their hopes and dreams?

- What are their financial goals?

It is also important that this part of the story directly addresses the primary problem you are going to solve—what is hurting them enough that they are going to seek out a financial advisor?

Next, you want to address what they want in a financial advisor. Consider these questions:

- How do they envision their financial picture changing with your help?

- What financial strategies do they seek, now and in the long term?

- What emotional benefit do they want from an advisory relationship? How will they feel as a result of working with you?

- What do they want your relationship to look like? How often will you meet? How will you guide and support them?

Finally, include their primary financial concerns. This can be the main problem you are trying to solve for them, along with other secondary thoughts that might be on their mind.

For example, an attorney who is burnt out in their career has the primary financial concern of wondering how long until they can quit their job and not go broke. A secondary concern might be wondering if they are paying too much in taxes.

Here are a few best practices to note as you work on your persona:

- Use a story format—as humans, we are wired to connect to something familiar. Help your prospects see themselves in the persona.

- Use their voice—how would they describe their problem if you were speaking to them? What language would they use?

- Don't use jargon—use simple, plain English to describe problems, needs, concerns, and solutions.

- Only include problems on their mind—don't introduce problems they may not be aware of yet, such as taxation of their future retirement income.

- Don't overload them with information—don't include information on services they will need in the future or the full menu of services you offer. Stick to what solutions will alleviate their immediate, primary financial concern.

- Stick to general situations—don't introduce any unusual circumstances just because you once had a client with that experience. Write a story that would be mostly true for most niche clients.

Once you have developed your persona, apply it to every marketing decision going forward. Again, if you ask, "Would my persona resonate with this?" and the answer is "no," move on.

You may find yourself struggling with the idea of working with just one persona, especially if you work mostly with couples versus individuals. For purposes of this exercise, though, develop only one persona. If you mostly work with couples, you should choose the person in the couple who most closely matches the niche or is most likely to take the lead in the relationship. You can include the spouse or partner in the persona backstory, but it is important that your persona represents just one person.

Once you have completed this exercise, you have officially defined your one client.

ONE PROBLEM

With your one client defined, it's time to figure out the one common problem your niche market faces. This can be a challenging exercise because clients often have many different problems: they need to organize their finances, they need someone to delegate their finances to, and they need to make sure they have enough money in retirement. But as we've touched on, that's not what we are looking for here. We are looking for one problem that everyone in your niche faces that is the most painful and the most urgent for them to solve. The one that makes them reach out to a financial advisor in the first place.

Here are some questions to ask yourself to discover this one problem:

- What keeps your niche up at night?

- What situation is your niche actively facing in the ninety days before they hire a financial advisor?

- What hurdle do they need to overcome to reach the ideal outcome they hope to achieve?

Here are some examples of problems a niche may be facing:

- Being able to plan for irregular income, so they aren't living a feast-or-famine lifestyle (e.g., commercial pilots, salespeople, business owners, attorneys, the self-employed)

- Facing such intense career burnout that they need to retire from their current high-paying careers as soon as possible (e.g., health-care professionals, tech employees, attorneys)

- Facing a significant tax bill in one year (e.g., selling a business, employees of a company who experienced an IPO, selling investment real estate)

- Needing to be solely responsible for a significant amount of wealth for the first time and not knowing where to start (e.g., inheritors, widows, divorcees)

- Needing to legitimize their finances to be able to qualify for credit cards, loans, and mortgages (e.g., legal sex workers, legal cannabis industry workers, under-the-table freelancers)

This problem needs to be top of mind for the niche. It needs to be distinct to the niche and not a problem most people face (e.g., planning for retirement). It needs to be painful enough that the niche will take action to solve it. And it is best if that problem needs to be urgently solved (though this is often not the case).

You want to avoid the following types of problems:

- Organizational problems. Unless you are going to position yourself as the Marie Kondo of wealth management, this is not a driving factor for someone hiring a financial advisor. It is an unforeseen benefit they enjoy but didn't know they needed.

- Planning for retirement. Literally, everyone has this problem except for the top 1 percent. If, as part of your niche, you are helping them plan for retirement, there needs to be some sort of complexity associated with it. For example, you are helping them plan for retirement by navigating the complex Federal Retirement System (FRS).

You may have to get creative with how you define the problem if your niche does not recognize it as painful or urgent enough to address. In some cases, you may have to turn something positive and frame it as a negative. For example, if your clients have more money than they'll ever need and want to optimize their wealth, you would want to turn around the aspirational goal to instead solve a problem, such as "stop fearing you are missing out on opportunities to further grow your wealth."

Of course, your clients will have more than the one problem you identify here. But once more, your marketing message does not need to say everything you do. That will just confuse your niche. It just needs to say the one thing that has been nagging at your prospect most.

ONE SOLUTION

Once you've articulated one problem your niche clients have, you need to have one solution that solves it. This is usually a proprietary process or some sort of unique service offering. At this stage, you probably don't have a unique solution for your niche. For now, you will use your existing financial planning process and just title it something that appeals to your niche. For example, "Aviators Income Stabilizer System." Or you can say how you deliver on solving this problem. For example, "we develop an equity compensation tax plan." This is one area you will develop as you've had more time and experience to work with your niche. I will discuss this more in Chapter 8.

ONE OUTCOME

Finally, we get to the one outcome. This is what your prospects hope to achieve after working with you. This is their highest, realistic aspiration. To get to this, we ask the following questions:

- What does your niche prospect want?

- How will the prospect transform after working with you?

- What will their life look like after working with you?

- What short-term success will your prospect achieve from working with you?

Take your answers and distill them down to one single outcome that directly resolves the one problem you identify.

Let's refer back to my original fictionalized client Chelsea, the commercial pilot. Her one problem is that "inconsistent income from having multiple jobs is stressful." Her one solution is "a system that helps pilots stabilize their monthly income." And the one outcome would be "living more like a nine-to-five person."

The key here is that the outcome be something the prospect can visualize and helps them see how their life will transform for the better. In our example, saying they can live like a nine-to-five person means they can live with more certainty and consistency, which will reduce their stress.

VISUAL BRAND

This chapter has so far focused entirely on your marketing message—the words you use to communicate to your niche how you can solve their problems. Your position is more than this, though. It is also comprised of your visual brand: the logo, colors, fonts, and images you use for your website, stationery (digital or print), marketing materials, and potentially even your office setting.

You will probably struggle to have a truly unique visual brand that stands out from the crowd. Unless you are especially creative or spend the big bucks to hire a top-notch branding agency, your brand will probably look fairly average or even below average. Prospects will overlook this if your message echoes exactly who they are and the challenges they are facing.

I'm not going to spend too much time on branding, but here are some general tips:

- If you are going to use images of people (which I recommend), they must look like your niche client.

- If your niche is people who value aesthetics (e.g., graphic designers, architects, interior designers, artists), spend money developing your visual brand. They will be more likely to judge a book by its cover and move on if they don't like your website.

- Use colors that appeal to your niche.

- Get a professional logo and website. While your visual brand doesn't have to be exceptional, you do want to instill confidence that you are a professional company.

- Don't make the brand about you. I know personal branding is and has been popular for a while, but people don't care about you; they only care about themselves. Unless you are trying to be an influencer, make the brand about your client.

- Make your brand reflect your niche.

Simply follow the general guidelines and you should have a brand that effectively pairs with a strong marketing message.

WHERE TO NEXT?

When positioning your firm, the mantra "less is more" applies. You will just turn off potential clients by overwhelming them with descriptions of everything you do to help them. Instead, keep your messaging simple: talk to your niche in their language, talk about the problem that keeps them up at night, and talk about how you will help them stop stressing about that problem. This approach takes work, but you will find the effort worthwhile. Once you have your marketing message, you are ready to start presenting it. In Chapter 5, you will learn about where to present it—your niche's community.

KEY TAKEAWAYS

- Once you have a niche, you need a marketing message. Your message should be clear, simple, and repeated constantly. This is the key to your message's success.

- You can write your message using the following formula: One Client + One Problem + One Solution + One Outcome. The client is your niche, the problem is what keeps them up at night, the solution is how you fix the problem, and the outcome is what they achieve in working with you.

- A persona will help keep your marketing on track. Once you have a persona, check all marketing decisions against it. If the marketing tactic would not resonate with your persona, discard it.

- If your visual brand is average or even slightly below average, most clients (except for the most aesthetically inclined, like graphic designers) will not care as long as your message speaks directly to them.

TOOLS

Persona Template
- Visit OnNiche.com/persona to create your own persona.

CHAPTER 5

Community

T o truly be a success within your niche, you must integrate into their community. You want to listen to others, contribute, and be part of the conversation.

The community is where your niche already congregates—this might include clubs, associations, events, or social media groups. Or the community might be found through the form of media they consume. While your niche doesn't congregate there, they are subscribers and are influenced by these sites and publications. Some communities may even be led by individuals. For example, they all follow one particular thought leader in their industry or on social media. This influencer is the ringleader of a community.

Your goal is to uncover what the community looks like to guide you on where to put your marketing efforts. Ask yourself where the prospective client is. The more targeted the group, the better. But that's not always possible. If you aren't sure where your niche is, just ask them for insight.

In Part 3 of this book, I will give you the specific details of when and how to engage your niche community. And I'll give you adaptations depending on what type of advisor you are. But for now, let's look at where you can find your niche community from a 10,000-foot view.

SOCIAL MEDIA

Most niches with a shared identity will congregate on social media or other online forums. It's your job to find where these people congregate. The right social media platform for you depends on your niche. Which ones do they use? Don't make the mistake of using the most popular or trendy sites if your niche is not there. Once you have found your niche on social media, here is how you want to participate.

Join Groups

Join groups where your niche is actively engaging and then become an active participant. This will give you a chance to interact with your niche directly. You will be able to "listen" and learn about the biggest challenges your niche faces. You'll also be able to contribute to the conversation. When participating in groups, come from the mindset that you are there to be a resource. Read the posts that are already in the group, and comment on those. Is there a way you can add value while showcasing your expertise at the same time? Be a contributor, not a self-promoter. The more you participate, the more you will be recognized in that group.

Follow Your Niche

As you get to know people in the groups, start to follow the personal accounts of individuals. Then react, comment, and share on their posts. This is a quick way for individuals to notice you. Even if the person is not following you back, you get on their radar. This may not work if they have hundreds of thousands of followers, but it will work for most individuals.

NETWORKING

Where can you interact with your niche face-to-face? Examples include conferences, events, community centers, networking groups, religious institutions, and peer groups (e.g., mastermind groups). Networking is one of the more immediate steps you can take to integrate into your niche community. The more people you meet, the more opportunities will develop. The word will spread faster the more people you know. And you will have more people added to your network whom you can continue to nurture.

Attend Events

Attend any conferences, workshops, meetups, mixers, or events your niche attends. In the beginning, there is no such thing as attending too many niche-focused events. Avoid any general networking events like the Chamber of Commerce or Rotary Clubs unless you can make a strong argument for attending.

Network Online

We've already talked about social media and community forums. If you are working with a national niche, though, online may be your only option for networking, and you'll want to explore it further.

Jane Mepham, the advisor whose niche is foreign-born residents and citizens who are dealing with cross-border money issues, networks online through a group called The CIGA Network, which brings together cross-border advisors from all around the world to support one another. Jane explains, "It's a place where I can reach out if I have questions for my clients that I haven't come across before."

Not all online networking will be obviously business related. For my fictional company Aviation Capital Management, the advisors who are pilots in the firm would network in online pilot communities as fellow pilots first and add expertise as a financial advisor when warranted.

Join Associations

Joining associations allows you to attend events where you can network with people in your niche. Some professional associations will allow you to join as an affiliated member if you provide services to their members. Or you can attend events as a guest. For example, when I first started my business, I would attend local financial advisor association networking events as a guest of a member. Once I was seen as a legitimate service provider within the financial services industry, I was able to join associations as an affiliated member.

In addition to being able to network at in-person events, many associations have online communities where you can network with members in between live events.

One final benefit of joining associations is that it shows commitment to your niche. Prospective clients will assume you are an expert in your niche, even as an outsider, because you have joined an association that supports that niche.

MEDIA

Media is all the content that your niche is already consuming. Media can be a great way to get in front of thousands of prospective clients at once. Even if it doesn't lead to new appointments immediately, it will create credibility that you are an expert in your field.

If you're working with professionals, this could include industry publications. If you are working with people of a similar affinity, then association publications may work. There is also traditional media such as newspapers, magazines, TV, or radio, as well as new media like podcasts or YouTube series. Remember, you are trying to find your community, so you are only going to identify content that your niche is currently consuming. Unless you are already established in your niche, you should not consider your own blog or podcast as media.

To integrate into the community via media, follow these guidelines.

Contribute Guest Blogs

Contribute guest blog posts to popular websites your niche visits. Many websites are in need of content but don't have the budget to pay for the writers to create it. See if you can contribute to niche-specific websites with the blogs you are already creating so that you aren't doing additional work. Sometimes, these sites will require you to provide original content. In this case, you can adjust a piece you have already created enough to make it original. Or you can write it from the opposite perspective (e.g., "Top Five Tips for Selling Your Business" becomes "Top Five Mistakes to Avoid When Selling Your Business"). By repurposing content you've already created, you are using less of your time.

You may sometimes be asked to pay to have your guest submission published. If you are new to the niche and the amount is nominal to your budget, I recommend paying the fee.

Contribute Articles

Contribute articles to publications your target market reads. This is very similar to the previous point, though print publications are harder to get into even if they have an online version. This is because they are usually subscription-based, so they have a higher threshold for quality than ad-based sites that need volume to attract readers.

If you have a hard time getting published in a publication, you may have to buy an advertorial (an ad that looks like an article). At a minimum, this usually will require a six-month commitment and thousands of dollars in advertising spend. Only do this if the publication is highly targeted to your niche and you don't need the advertorial to have an immediate ROI for it to be worth it to you.

Be a Guest on a Podcast

Be a guest on a podcast your niche listens to. This can be a great way to use media because once you are on one podcast, you are often asked to be on another. Podcasts that have an interview format are often in need of guests, so they look to see who else has been on similar podcasts. It also provides more content for you to share, adds credibility, and the podcast host will share it with their audience. Plus, it will take very little of your time and build a relationship with the podcast host. It's a win across the board.

Get Quoted by Reporters

If you can't get your articles published in the publications you want, see if you can get quoted in an article instead. There are sites like Help a Reporter Out (HARO.com) and some associations like the National Association of Personal Financial Advisors (NAPFA) that will send requests for interviews, so you can find opportunities related to your niche. Be careful, though, not to set your expectations too high for results. This is usually a way to gain credibility within your niche, it may lead to other opportunities, and it can help with search engine optimization for your own site. But rarely does being quoted directly lead to new clients.

Influencers

Influencers are people who are the gatekeepers to your niche. They are the people who already have the audience you want to reach, and likely have built-in trust and authority within this network. These are not the traditional centers of influence we talk about in the industry, like Certified Public Accountants (CPAs) and attorneys who can refer clients. While centers of influence are important people in your network, most of them will not be the gatekeeper to thousands of people in your niche.

Influencers need to have access and influence over large populations of your niche. This can be either online or offline. One boutique RIA I work with has a specialty in families with adult children with serious mental health issues. In this case, the staff members working at various mental health nonprofits are influencers. They have direct understanding, access, and influence with the families he wants to reach. They are able to connect the firm to this audience by inviting the CEO to speak to national, regional, and local association events.

Leveraging these relationships with others will be the fastest way to get in front of your desired audience. This does not mean referrals. While this would be a great secondary benefit, developing the trust to get a referral takes time. Plus, trying to generate referrals from influencers is thinking too small. Influencers should have networks of thousands of people in your niche. They have a built-in network that they can help you get in front of.

Here are ways to leverage influencers:

- Engage on Social Media: Engage with influencers your niche follows on social media. By commenting on their posts, they may start to follow what you are doing as well. At the very least, you'll get on their radar. In the best-case scenario, they will share your content with their network or invite you to contribute to the work they are doing.

- Contribute Content: Ask to contribute your expertise to the work your influencer is already doing. Do they have a newsletter or website? Ask to contribute a guest post. Do they organize events? Ask to be a panelist or guest speaker and offer to invite your own network as well. Do they have a podcast with guests? Offer to be a guest on their show.

THE REWARDS OF COMMUNITY

The quicker you integrate into your niche's community, the quicker you will see prospective clients schedule appointments. You will also find rewards beyond securing new clients. You will develop insights into your niche that other advisors lack, and you may find it gratifying to know you are helping people by sharing your expertise with them. I will cover this expertise in the next chapter.

KEY TAKEAWAYS

- You need to integrate into your niche's community to get them to notice and work with you.

- To get on your niche's radar, you can focus on social media, networking, media, and influencers. Each of these areas offers opportunities to learn about your niche and focus your marketing efforts.

- Ask yourself where your niche is. You may feel tempted to try trendy venues, such as the latest social media site. But if your niche isn't congregating there, you only waste your time. Focus on the places, both online and in person, where you can truly connect with your niche.

- Get involved with the community as much as possible. Be helpful by answering questions without promoting yourself. Write articles or be a podcast guest. Contribute content to influencers and provide quotes for reporters. The faster you can get your niche's attention and respect, the better it is for your business.

CHAPTER 6

Expertise

To earn credibility within your niche market, you need to demonstrate your expertise in working with clients like them. Making these claims through your website, marketing materials, or sales pitches is not sufficient. A more effective and sustainable approach is to demonstrate your expertise through content marketing.

Content marketing is defined as "a strategic marketing approach focused on creating and distributing valuable, relevant, and consistent content to attract and retain a clearly defined audience—and, ultimately, to drive profitable customer action."[9]

Content can include blogs, articles, podcasts, emails, videos, webinars, presentations, and eBooks, just to name a few. Content marketing is the foundation of a niche marketing strategy and has a variety of benefits:

---

9   "What Is Content Marketing?" Content Marketing Institute, accessed February 20, 2023, https://contentmarketinginstitute.com/what-is-content-marketing.

- It builds your reputation as an expert in your niche, demonstrates your authority, and builds trust.

- It provides buy-in from your prospects, so your sales process is easier and your close rate is higher.

- It attracts prospects to you instead of you having to go find them.

- It improves your search rankings and drives organic traffic to your website.

While content marketing is the medium you will use to become the expert, the expertise process begins with learning.

LEARN EVERYTHING

When you commit to a niche, you are committing to being a lifelong learner of that niche. Not only do you have to keep on top of the basic news, laws, and trends of the financial services industry, but you also have to stay on top of the news and trends of your niche. By learning everything you can, you also learn to speak their language—the words they use to talk to other people in their niche. Learning their language is key to being accepted as part of the niche community.

This language should be reflected back to them in all the content marketing you create, helping you connect with your niche market as they feel like you are talking specifically to them.

When you first start out in your niche, dedicate time each week to studying. Each niche is different, so the information and channels to follow will be different. You may need to interview other professionals serving your niche, read industry publications, listen to community podcasts, or attend professional events. For example, if your niche is employees of a specific company or industry, read all the industry news, learn everything you can about the companies in that industry, and learn the ins and outs of the benefit packages offered. If your niche is widows, interview estate planning attorneys, read blogs and listen to podcasts focused on widows, learn all the steps and laws that widows will be impacted by, and attend estate planning association events.

In the early days, and as you become more established in your niche, learning as much as possible will serve you well. What you learn will serve as the basis for the content you will create.

For Bruce Barton, continuing education has become ingrained in his company culture. Silicon Valley, and the tech industry in general, is always on the cutting edge of everything from the products they build to the company cultures they create. And that goes for innovation in equity compensation as well.

"We have to stay up to date on all the rules, requirements, regulations, and tax laws regarding equity compensation, including incentive stock options, non-qualified stock options, restricted stock units [RSUs], performance shares, and startup company founder's stock," he explains. "Companies continue to innovate; for example, large private companies now issue 'double-trigger RSUs' to solve an income tax problem for their employees."

When you are dealing with such technical issues, you have to stay educated about the latest changes because they can have serious financial consequences for your clients. But this intense learning requirement will also make it easier to protect your niche from other advisors.

If you are truly aiming to be uncomparable, dedication to early and continued learning is required to serve your niche to your highest ability. You must know everything there is to know about your niche.

CREATE CONTENT

Depending on your situation, you may have very little experience working with your niche, or you may have years of it. No matter how much knowledge or experience you have, you must market yourself as an expert within your niche. The goal is to have prospects who have no connection to your firm be attracted to and evaluate your firm based on your expertise.

The best way to convey this expertise is not by merely stating you are an expert in your niche on your website. Instead, you must demonstrate your expertise through content that is relevant to your niche. A well-thought-out content strategy will help you begin to position yourself as a thought leader.

Creating content is important in your niche marketing journey because

- The research required will build your knowledge, skills, and confidence when working with your niche

- It will help you articulate your value

- You will be able to get feedback to see what resonates and what doesn't for future marketing campaigns

- When people see your content, you begin to establish a reputation as an expert

There are dozens of ways you can communicate your expertise through content. In the beginning, the key is to pick just one method and focus on that. As you master one, you may decide to layer on another.

I'm not going to go through all the possible content ideas. Instead, I'm going to recommend the ones I have seen that are the most beneficial over the long term—the ones that accomplish several objectives at once and can work for you year after year.

These content options may feel overwhelming. Remember, you don't need to do all of this, and you don't need to do it all at once. In Part 3 of this book, I will guide you as to which content mediums to focus on in each year of your journey, as well as the frequency. You also don't need to do this alone. Content marketing is one area where you can leverage technology and outsource to professionals to help you.

Blog

The content format I recommend advisors start with is a blog. Writing helps you fully develop your thoughts around the challenges your niche is facing and the solutions you are offering. It forces you to articulate the issues and language of your niche. And it builds credibility, establishing you as an expert with your niche.

Blogs should always highlight your knowledge and expertise with your niche so that readers know you solve the problems of people just like them.

Even if your niche doesn't read blogs, the content will help prospects find your website through search engines like Google, which can end up being a significant source of leads. Having niche-specific blogs on your website also reinforces that you are an expert with that niche . . . even if they just glance at the title.

Blogs are one of the easiest forms of content to be shared on other websites or print publications that cater to your niche. It's unlikely that a reputable publication will share a video or podcast episode you created, but there is a chance they will publish a guest blog. In the beginning, you may not have built a large network of niche contacts, so leveraging platforms that already have your audience will help expand your reach.

If you don't have the skills or the desire to write these yourself from scratch, you have a couple of options. First, AI technology can help you create an outline or even a first draft of a blog that you can then expand on or customize to your niche. Second, you can hire a ghostwriter to write content for you. If you use either option, you'll want to make sure your unique expertise with a niche is evident. You don't want to end up with generic content.

Podcast

When you host a podcast, a certain level of expertise is inherently implied. No one would assume you would spend the time, money, and energy hosting and producing a podcast if you weren't an expert. Since it is expected, a podcast immediately elevates you to this status.

There are two commonly used format options for advisor podcasts. The first is the solo host, where you are talking to the audience the entire time on a selected topic. If you are not a skilled entertainer, this format is not advised. It takes a tremendous amount of time and effort to prepare for each episode, and you must be skilled enough to keep it entertaining so that people want to listen not only to one episode but to many of them.

The second format is to be the host and interview a guest for each episode. While it takes more coordination to find, invite, and prepare guests, there is much less overall preparation that goes into each episode. Having a guest-based show also presents an opportunity to reach out to centers of influence in your niche. Most professionals will accept the invitation to be a guest on your podcast because they see it as free marketing for their services to your audience. If they don't have a business they are promoting, they may just enjoy telling their story.

Start by inviting professionals in your existing network to be guests. Once you have a track record, you can reach out to cold centers of influence and ask them to be a guest. This can overlap with your center of influence strategy that will be discussed in Chapter 7. When the guest says yes, you now have several touch-point opportunities to deepen the relationship: First is the initial invitation. Second is to have a pre-interview before the podcast to prepare them for the show. Third is to record the podcast. Fourth is to follow up when the podcast has been published.

Matt Halloran of podcasting company ProudMouth coaches his advisor clients to have a stipulation for guests that they must share the episode with their network through sharing it on their social media networks, posting it to their website, or sending it out to their email list. This ends up being a free promotion of your business and expands the reach of your podcast.

Your guests don't just have to be traditional centers of influence. They can also be influencers in your niche community—for example, authors who have written books your niche is interested in or podcast hosts your niche listens to. They can also just be people your niche is interested in. If you work with pilots, a guest could be a legendary pilot in the aviation world.

You may be thinking, "What if no one listens to my podcast?" Don't worry about that. If literally no one listened to your podcast, it would still be worthwhile because

1. You are immediately viewed as an expert

2. You use it as an opportunity to connect and nurture relationships with centers of influence

3. Your guests will promote your business to their audience

If you end up with a loyal following, you'll see even more benefits from a podcast. When prospects listen to your voice episode after episode, intimacy forms. You are joining them during their personal times such as exercising, cooking, driving, or even lying in bed—not places you normally would be able to market to them.

While you can learn how to create a podcast from any number of YouTube videos, if you have an established business, you would be better served hiring freelancers or a professional podcast company to handle the production.

Presentations

There is no quicker way to position yourself as an expert than to present your expertise in front of a group. So that you are always ready to fill in as a last-minute speaker, develop a presentation that can be altered to various lengths (e.g., fifteen minutes, thirty minutes, forty-five minutes, sixty minutes). This presentation should be easily presented either virtually or in person.

The key to an effective marketing presentation is to make sure it reinforces your brand message of one client + one problem + one solution + one outcome. In other words, it should address your niche's primary pain points, and the solutions should reflect the process you would take them through if they were a client.

For the fictitious Aviation Capital Management focused on commercial pilots, the presentation would be "Five Steps to Stabilizing Income for Commercial Pilots." It would introduce one problem, which is that inconsistent income from multiple jobs is stressful. It would walk through the solution to this problem by listing the steps the advisor guides her clients through to solve this problem, such as budgeting, cash management, savings, and investing. And it would forecast what outcome the audience can expect if they successfully implement the steps—living like a nine-to-five person.

The goal of the presentation is to presell your audience on what you do. The biggest mistake I see advisors make when creating presentations is choosing the wrong topic. Often the topic does not represent how the advisor primarily helps them.

I once spoke to an advisor specializing in widows and divorcees who faced this issue. She had been presenting on the topic of estate planning at a local continuing education center for seniors. The class consistently sold out each time she taught it, but she was not converting attendees into sales appointments, let alone into clients. When I asked her if people who attended her class could hire her to take them through just the steps she presented in her class, she said only if they became full wealth management clients. And even then, an estate planning attorney had to be involved. She was presenting on a problem that was not the primary problem she helps her clients solve. Instead of signing up attendees for prospect calls, the estate planning attorney in the room got most of the leads.

Make sure your presentation is on the one primary problem your niche faces that you solve. You can address other problems when you speak to them individually.

Books

Similar to a podcast and presenting to a group, a book immediately establishes you as an expert. Anyone who takes the time to write a book on a topic must be an expert.

At the risk of sounding like a broken record, your book should address the primary pain point your niche faces, and the solutions should reflect how your business works with clients. A book should help you with the following:

- Establish you as an expert

- Presell prospects into your process

- Create opportunities to connect with influential people in your niche

- Create additional marketing opportunities, such as speaking engagements and media opportunities

Once a book is published, you can leverage it to schedule speaking engagements or podcast appearances. It presents opportunities to be interviewed by the media, and your status is instantly elevated in your niche community.

Your book can also be used as a direct lead generator. You can send free copies to everyone in your niche community. You can even have it on your website to gather contact information from prospects in return for mailing them a free copy.

You don't even have to wait for the book to be fully written and published to see immediate marketing benefits from writing it. You can "cold call" prospects and influencers in your niche and ask to interview them for your book. You can then ask those people to introduce you to others in the niche they think you should interview. And you can interview other experts (a.k.a. centers of influence) for your book. Whether you quote them or not, include their names in the acknowledgments and send them a free copy (or more to give away). You now have built-in promoters to spread the word about your book.

As you are writing the book, you can repurpose portions of the content as blogs and share it as an "excerpt from your upcoming book." You can also use it as an excuse to reach out to prospects in your niche to be beta readers and provide feedback, such as asking experts to review specific chapters to confirm accuracy when you have a solid draft completed. All of these steps help engage your prospects and centers of influence throughout the book-writing process.

For financial advisor Allen Giese (the owner of a boutique RIA), bringing his expertise into a niche and, ultimately, a book changed the trajectory of his career.

From personal experience with his own son's diagnosis of mental illness, he knew the financial consequences these families faced all too well. Families with adult children who suffer from serious mental illness face the very serious stress of not only having to save enough money to last the rest of their lives but also the rest of their child's life.

One day, while participating in a fundraiser for a national mental health association, a fellow volunteer began asking Allen for advice about Achieving a Better Life Experience (ABLE) accounts and how his child could qualify for Medicaid. The two decided to meet later at Allen's office. Having never thought about these issues, even for his own situation, Allen began researching this information for his friend and quickly realized there was a lot more to planning for the long-term care of children who suffer from mental illness than he first thought. It became clear that parents would have to save a lot more money than the average couple by the time they reached retirement if they wanted to provide for their child when they were gone. He realized these people had a unique and complex situation he could personally connect with and felt passionate about helping. He had found his niche! And he began pursuing it.

While at a CEG Worldwide Roundtable event, Allen started talking to one of the vendors, now called Scribe Media. He described the experience to me: "I'm looking at the example books they published, and I thought, 'Damn, those are nice.' The price seemed fairly reasonable. I calculated how many million-dollar clients I would need to get from the book to make it pay for itself, which was about three. Would a book give me an advantage of at least three clients? Absolutely. I was completely sold."

Six months later, Allen's book, *When Mental Illness Strikes: Crisis Intervention for the Financial Plan*, was published. And he was quickly able to parlay that into speaking engagements.

To kick-start his speaking career, Allen bought a booth at a big disability convention in Orlando and at another smaller event which allowed him a speaking slot. From there, the word was out, and speaking requests began to flow in.

"A typical scenario today," he said, "is that someone in a therapy group will read my book and tell everybody else in the group, 'You've got to read this book.' The whole group reads the book, and then someone from the group will call and ask, 'Would you speak to our group? We meet Sunday nights at eight.'"

These virtual groups can have fifty or more people scattered all across the United States. And they happen regularly. Allen is also getting opportunities from unlikely sources. "There's this doctor who is influential in the mental health community, who now uses my book in his sessions. All of his patients know me, so I get calls from them. Recently someone from the doctor's office asked if I can speak to a group of all of his patients."

All these speaking engagements are on top of the national and regional conferences he speaks at for a national mental illness association.

Allen's experience shows just how powerful a book can be. And if you're ready for the investment of time (and almost certainly money), there are plenty of professionals who can help you. Just remember, though, (like with blogs) if you hire a ghostwriter, you need to work with them closely to ensure all of your expertise reaches the page.

Videos

Videos are another option for creating content that establishes your expertise. For those who can't or don't want to write, this is usually their go-to option for content creation. You can do

- A standard video blog, which usually is on a specific topic or a frequently asked question and lasts from thirty seconds to a few minutes

- Short-form videos created directly on social media platforms

- Video case studies for specific scenarios you come across within that niche market and the steps taken to get to a solution

- Live streams where you discuss a topic, take questions and answers, or provide commentary on a current event

- Creative thirty- to sixty-minute live webinars

- More extensive training, such as a multipart course over a duration of several weeks

- Whiteboard videos drawing out specific concepts

Videos should be educational, inspiring, or entertaining. If your niche consumes a lot of content on YouTube or other video-based social media platforms and you have a natural affinity for video, you can start to establish a reputation quickly.

I would warn most advisors to not start with videos if they are inexperienced with the medium. I find most can't pull this off because they either don't have the personality or the production skills to make it work. Successful videos often require creativity or an entertainment angle which is not always an advisor skill set.

Advisors may struggle to create videos with the consistency they need to make an impact.

It also takes a lot of effort to drive people to your videos. Your niche has to find it, so you have to spend time building up an audience or hoping the algorithms will work in your favor.

When you are starting a niche, the best thing you can do is leverage the audience of other people and platforms. It is not good to spend time building your own audience from scratch by trying to be a YouTube star or social media influencer. If you have an audience that consumes videos, and you can do a great job creating them, great. Give it a try. If not, though, your effort might be better focused elsewhere first.

GENERATE TOPIC IDEAS

Initially, you may find it difficult to come up with topics for your content marketing. The best topics are the ones that directly address your niche's primary pain points—the ones answering the questions that are top of mind and keep them up at night. Focus on things that your niche is curious about or even afraid of. And consider topics that would be top of mind for your prospect within ninety days of hiring you.

For example, if your niche is divorce financial planning, consider the issues on a prospect's mind before hiring a financial advisor to help with their divorce. For example, it could be "Why Getting Half Isn't Always Financially Fair in a Divorce." If your niche is people who have received an inheritance, a topic could be "Common Tax Mistakes People Make with Their Inheritance."

Help your niche understand that the content is specifically for them by inserting them into the title. If you address retirement planning for business owners, then you can tailor the title to be "Three

Mistakes Business Owners Make When Selling Their Business That Can Damage Their Retirement Plans."

Whatever you do, do not include generic topics, such as economic outlooks. Every subject must be specific to your niche, use their language, and provide examples that resonate with them. If you must write about a generic topic that applies to any investor, tailor the topic title and examples to your niche.

Choosing topics when you first work with a niche can be challenging. As you gain more experience, it will become easier to find issues to address. To help do this, take notes about the situations your prospects face. Your notes will tell you exactly what you should discuss in your content.

Specifically, here are the things to make note of.

Triggering Events

What event was happening in the prospect's life that triggered them to reach out to you in the first place? In the example about women getting a divorce, the triggering event could be finding out a spouse is cheating, talking to a divorce attorney, filing for a divorce, or going through a divorce and having the gut feeling she isn't getting a fair settlement. These are just four different triggering scenarios; I'm sure there are many more.

Primary Financial Concerns

What does the prospect say their primary financial concern or frustration is? For a divorcing woman, her primary concern may be, "Will I have enough money to maintain the lifestyle for myself and the kids that we are all used to?"

Goals and Aspirations

What does the prospect say is their ultimate goal or aspiration? What would they like to achieve after working with you? For the divorcing woman, she may say her goal is to rebuild a life on her terms where she feels happy, confident, and secure.

Services and Solutions

What services or solutions does the prospect say they need? Make note of these, even if they are not services you offer. For example, the divorcing woman may need to refinance the house in her name. You note that she may need mortgage services, and you write content on refinancing a home as part of a divorce settlement.

Words and Phrases

What specific words and phrases does the prospect use to describe their situation? It will be important to reflect this wording back to your niche in your content. For example, the divorcing woman may say she needs to "refinance" her home, but she also may instead say she needs to lower her mortgage payment or get her husband's name off the mortgage. These would be key phrases to write down that you could use as a topic. The topic, in this case, would be "How to Lower Your Monthly Mortgage Payments So You Can Afford to Keep Your House after a Divorce." Avoid using financial services industry jargon. Instead, use the language your niche clients would use.

SHARE YOUR CONTENT

Once you are developing content on a consistent basis, you'll want to share this content with your niche. You can do this through many of the channels I discussed in Chapter 5 about integrating into your community, especially social media and media categories. In addition, in Chapter 7, you'll learn how to share it with the personal network you will develop.

ACHIEVE THOUGHT LEADERSHIP

When you adopt the habit of learning and creating content, you will eventually develop your own thoughts regarding the problems and solutions your niche faces instead of regurgitating what you have learned. Because solving the problems of your niche is what you think about day in and day out, you begin to come up with creative processes or solutions that no one has thought of before. You think of new frameworks for solving your niche's problems. You become a thought leader.

Thought leadership and content overlap but are different. **Thought leadership is when you are recognized by others in your niche as an expert. Developing content is the process to get you there, but thought leadership is determined by others.** At the thought leadership level, you are an invited speaker to events, you are quoted in publications, you have a large number of subscribers who voluntarily opted into your newsletter list, you have a TV or radio show, you write a book, or you have a popular podcast.

Now, some things can be bought instead of earned. But even purchased thought leadership is only effective if people are actually listening to what you have to say. To achieve thought leadership, you must have a consistent history of valuable content that many people follow.

CONTENT MAKES YOU UNCOMPARABLE

Creating content can feel onerous, especially since it must be ongoing to succeed. However, content is the foundation for your credibility and eventual thought leadership. When you are perceived as the expert in your niche is when you truly become uncomparable.

You will not create content in a vacuum. As you establish your credibility, you also build your network of people to share content with. Chapter 7 covers the importance of your network and how to nurture it.

KEY TAKEAWAYS

- Demonstrating your expertise is foundational to attracting your niche. You can do this by creating content that your niche finds valuable and relevant.

- By consistently creating content, you build your reputation, demonstrate authority, build trust with your niche, gain their buy-in, attract prospects, improve search ranking, and drive visitors to your website.

- Content methods include blogs, podcasts, presentations, books, and videos. Finding ideas to discuss may be difficult at first, but take notes about what your prospects talk about, and use your notes to generate content topics.

- When you consistently create content, you start to see creative solutions and processes for helping your niche. You become recognized as an expert and achieve thought leadership.

CHAPTER 7

Network

Anetwork is similar to, but not to be confused with, a community. The community is where your niche congregates. You may know some of the people in the niche community, but you won't know the vast majority of them. A network, on the other hand, is the people you know or who know you. These are the people who have opted in to build a relationship with you on some level, even if that just means following you on social media or being subscribed to your newsletter.

Think of the difference like this. You belong to a social media group composed of your niche: self-employed creative professionals. There may be twenty-five thousand people in that group. That is your community. But through your interactions in the group, twenty-five people have subscribed to your newsletter, and one hundred have friended you on social media. Those people are in your network.

Building your network is important to your overall strategy because these are the people who will become clients, share your content, present you with new marketing opportunities, or refer

business to you. Your network can be composed of current and prospective clients, referral partners (e.g., COIs), and influencers. As you build a large network and nurture it over a period of years, this is primarily where your flow of leads will come from.

HOW TO BUILD YOUR NETWORK

Building your network (and, as a result, your database) will be one of the most valuable things you can do in your niche strategy. It is an asset that will pay dividends for years to come.

Financial advisor Eric Sigdestad (the owner of a boutique RIA) summed up his strategy for the first years of working with his niche of employees of a specific telecommunications company.

"I focused on getting as many niche leads into my database as I could as quickly as possible. Once the leads were in our database, it got easier. The marketing at that point was all about nurturing those relationships through various touchpoints. It could take a lead several years to schedule an appointment, so building our database early on yielded appointments in future years."

In the early years of his business, Eric had to get creative to get these leads. He would set up an In-N-Out Burger truck across the street from the utility company's location, then lure the employees out by offering them a free cheeseburger if they filled out a postcard with their contact information. Once he got their names, the nurturing system would begin.

"At the beginning, we'd get a lot of leads. Eventually, we got the names of almost everyone in the building. While it did help us get names into our system, and a lot of people became clients, it did have its downsides. As we kept going back in, we weren't known for our acumen or fiduciary stewardship. We were known as the In-N-Out hamburger people, but I've been called worse."

You don't have to be known as the next hamburger people to build your network. But you need to make an effort to constantly build it. Your network will be built from the activities you engage in with the community. As you meet people, here's how you start to build your network.

Connect with Everyone on Social Media

Connect with everyone you meet in your niche on the platform where they are most likely to engage with you. For example, if your niche is attorneys, you can connect on LinkedIn. If your niche is interior designers, you could connect on Instagram. Your contacts will see your content and will remain top of mind. You should also comment and engage with them. And in return, they will engage with you.

Add Everyone to Your Email List

Anytime you exchange email addresses with someone, either online or in person, add them to your newsletter list. Just make sure you review your local regulations regarding email marketing rules to understand what is allowed and what is prohibited.

Offer a Lead Magnet

Most people who become aware of your business and are curious about what you do aren't yet ready to do business. You need a way to capture their names and contact information so you can nurture the relationship until they are ready to schedule an appointment.

The simplest way to do this is by offering a PDF resource like an eBook or checklist. You can also consider an on-demand webinar using the same presentation you are using to present to groups. There are also online tools offered by various technology vendors, though many of these will be too generic to appeal to your niche. The important thing is that the resource is something your niche will value and that you offer it in exchange for their email address.

This is where creativity can come in too. Just get those leads. Once you have their contact information, these people are officially part of your network that you should start nurturing.

HOW TO NURTURE YOUR NETWORK

Once you have collected names, you need to consistently nurture those relationships for years to come. Dealing with personal finances is not enjoyable for most prospective clients. It may take them years before the problem they have is so painful or so urgent that they finally seek out a financial advisor. You want to nurture these relationships so that when they do finally take action, you are the one who comes top of mind. Let's look at ways to accomplish this.

Email Newsletter

An email marketing list is the most valuable marketing asset you own. Once someone is on your list, you have the opportunity to continue to market to them in the future. Sending emails to a robust list of truly interested and engaged prospects is the most effective form of marketing.

The reason an email marketing list is so valuable is that it is the one thing you own and can control. You own the email addresses, you decide the content you send, and you decide the date, time, and frequency to send your content.

An email newsletter is the easiest form of email marketing because it promotes the content you are already creating to showcase your expertise. Whether you are creating blogs, videos, or podcasts, you can share that same content with everyone on your email marketing list through your newsletter.

A newsletter reinforces your expertise and establishes credibility with your niche. When your newsletter features topics showcasing your expertise with a niche, it won't take long for people to also believe in your expertise. The newsletter will help you stay top of mind with your audience on a regular basis. Even if someone is not opening your email, they see your name. At some point, you hope they remember your name when they finally decide to seek expert help.

Social Media

A second way to nurture your network is to post your original content on social media. While you may not get a lot of engagement right away, as you connect with people, it will be a way to stay top of mind with your connections. I recommend making sure that the title of the content you are sharing makes it obvious that you work with a specific niche. That way, you are reinforcing that message even if someone is just scrolling past your post.

Don't forget to use social media as a center of influence nurturing tool. I find that using it to nurture influencers who hold the key to more marketing opportunities or referrals is the best use of time on social media. Nurturing one-off prospects from social media is time-consuming, but nurturing relationships that can give you more access to your niche will pay dividends for years to come.

In addition to creating and sharing your own content, you can curate the content of others and share it with your network. This will demonstrate your interest in and commitment to your niche. Spend some time each week searching for content that your niche would be interested in. Release it on your social media profiles throughout the week. Consider curating content from people who are influencers and tag them in your posts because now your content is doing double duty. It is nurturing your broader social media network as well as your relationship with the individual influencer.

Drip Emails

When you first add a new person to your network, especially through a marketing campaign like a lead magnet, you want to have an accelerated nurturing process to see if they'll take action right away. You do this through a series of emails that are automatically sent over a period of weeks based on when the contact was added to your marketing database. While most people won't take action during this period, there will be some who are primed to set an appointment immediately. For the people who do not take action, you will continue to nurture them through your email newsletter.

Events

Hosting live or virtual events—either social or educational—can help deepen the relationship with your network. You can also promote your events to the wider niche community in the hopes they attend and transition to being a part of your network.

Events for a niche are different from the traditional lunch and learns or client appreciation events most advisors host. Every topic must be uniquely tailored to the interests of the niche. For example, if you work with newly divorced women who traditionally put their husband's and children's interests ahead of their own, you could host an event focused on self-care. You can have a nutritionist and an aesthetician as guest speakers. If you are focused on impact investing, you can have an event with lesser-known, forward-thinking nonprofits who share their stories.

Not only do these events nurture the people in your network who attend, but it also nurtures relationships with speakers. It's good to primarily choose speakers who will be able to give you more access to your niche. Even if your event is not a huge success, building a relationship with the speakers alone can make it worthwhile.

One caveat is that events can be quite risky. Live events are often expensive, and if you don't have as many people attend as you intended, you could end up feeling embarrassed. In the beginning, stick to virtual events or intimate events where you only expect ten to twelve people, and you know you can deliver on that. Expand the event size as your events gain momentum.

Meet One-on-One

I know it's old school, but having one-on-one conversations still works. It builds rapport and can be a source for other marketing opportunities you might not have thought of yet.

One-on-one can take so many forms. You can have a meal together or just enjoy coffee or cocktails. You can play a round of golf or invite someone to a concert. If you are in a national niche, you may not have the luxury to meet with people face-to-face, but in this case, you can still schedule thirty-minute phone or video calls.

Referrals

This should come as no surprise, but one benefit to nurturing your network is to generate referrals. Most advisory firms have no problem generating referrals from clients. In fact, that is how many generalist firms grow—through positive word of mouth from existing clients.

There are a million and one resources available to financial advisors for generating referrals from your clients and centers of influence, so I'm not going to describe them here. But when you have a specialty working with a niche, all of those strategies you've heard experts lecture about over the years become more effective. It's easier for clients and COIs to refer because they understand whom you serve, the problems you can solve, and the overall value you bring to the table.

A POWERFUL TOOL IN YOUR UNCOMPARABLE FRAMEWORK

As a financial advisor, you might already be a networking expert. The difference now is that your network becomes more focused yet has greater reach. Your network becomes an invaluable tool to spread your message supported by all the other areas of the Uncomparable Framework—including your business model, which is covered in Chapter 8.

KEY TAKEAWAYS

- Your network constitutes the people you nurture, sometimes over years, so that they become clients, share your content, present marketing opportunities, and refer business to you.

- Focus on building a network early. You do this by connecting with your niche on social media, adding everyone possible to your email list, and offering a resource such as an eBook in exchange for contact information.

- Nurture your network, knowing that it can take years before someone will schedule an appointment. An email newsletter keeps you top of mind while reinforcing your expertise. You can also nurture your network through social media, drip emails, events (live or virtual), and one-on-one meetings.

CHAPTER 8

Business Model

Advisors who successfully develop a niche practice design all aspects of their business to serve that niche. Their entire business model is built with the ideal niche client in mind. When you fully commit to your niche, it will not only dictate your brand, the message you communicate, and the content you create but also the processes you employ, the services you offer, the technology you use, and the staff you hire. Let me give you an example of what it truly means to niche.

I have worked with many firms that describe their ideal client as business owners, fifty-five to sixty-five years old, within five years of retirement, who are delegators, and who have at least $1 million in investable assets, with more assets coming in after the sale of their business.

Yet some of these firms will offer their standard retirement planning and investment management services to these business owners. There really isn't much the firm does differently for business owners than they do for their other clients—the client just happens to be a business owner. The presentations they give are all on general economic and financial topics that would really appeal to a mass market. While these firms have a clear idea of whom they want to work with, I wouldn't consider them to be truly focused on a niche because they haven't designed their business around their niche.

In contrast, there are other firms that design their entire service offering around business owners. They offer business valuation services and exit strategies in addition to investment management and financial planning. Their process and services are intentionally designed to meet the unique needs of their niche. They bring in speakers specific to the topics business owners care about, such as business succession planning options. They make introductions to business brokers who can help list their business. They subscribe to software that allows them to calculate a basic business valuation each year to see how the business owner client is progressing toward their goals. And they hire staff who are also passionate about small business. Business owners receive greater value from advisors in this second scenario because the solutions are specifically tailored to their needs and concerns. These firms have centered their entire business model on their niche, and it shows.

So how do you develop a business model tailored to the exact needs of your niche? You do it by focusing on four elements:

1. Proprietary Process

2. Client Experience

3. Services

4. Pricing

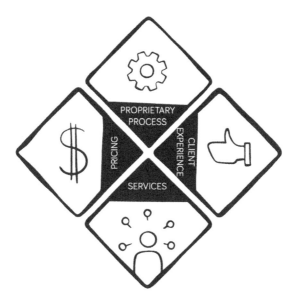

When you combine a proprietary process with a focus on a niche client experience, services, and pricing, you have an uncomparable business model.

PROPRIETARY PROCESS

You are selling the intangible, which can be hard for prospects to get their heads around. Establishing and defining a process can help your prospects understand what they are getting when they work with you.

If you want to become uncomparable, it needs to appear that you have a different process from what other financial advisors offer. That means adapting the Certified Financial Planner (CFP) Board's Financial Planning Process to make it sound like a proprietary version designed for your niche.

First, let's define what a proprietary process is. This process is the unique path that your company follows to achieve transformative results for your clients. Of course, most RIAs take their clients through the CFP Board's Financial Planning Process, but your proprietary process should stand out from the crowd because it is customized for your niche.

Why is it important to develop a proprietary process?

- **It empowers you.** Having a proprietary process gives you more confidence when you talk about your business and lets you communicate your message in a more articulate and thought-provoking way. This not only impacts how people receive your message but also how you deliver your message. With this process in place, you draw upon your own story and the deep aspects of who you are.

- **You will attract more clients.** Your proprietary process gives you a story to tell, and it creates a personal connection with people when you talk about your business. As you begin to speak to people about your process, your story will resonate with them.

- **You can charge higher prices.** A proprietary process instantly sets your business apart from your competition, which allows you to charge higher prices because they can't get what you have anywhere else. They won't be able to compare apples to oranges.

- **It makes presenting easier and more effective.** A proprietary process helps you outline your keynote presentation and provides a framework to clearly deliver your ideas from the stage in a way that makes your audience want to engage with you more.

Your proprietary process will take a client from where they are when they first come to you with their pain point to some outcome when you solve their initial problem. For marketing purposes only, your proprietary process is not going to include the ongoing maintenance of the relationship. You want your proprietary process to solve the one problem you defined and deliver at least the first stage of transformation. The ongoing relationship will be what comes after this process. I will show you an example of how this works shortly.

I recommend that you develop your proprietary process only after you have worked with dozens of niche clients. You need to have enough real-world experience to draw from in order to brainstorm an informed process.

When you start brainstorming about your proprietary process, start with the beginning and the end in mind. When your niche client first comes to you, ask yourself the following:

- What is their situation?

- What was their primary pain point?

Next, focus on the end result:

- What end result did they achieve?

- What transformation did they experience?

Then, fill in all the steps in between. Reflect on your process and the transformation you took your ideal client through. What are the steps that help them achieve their objective? Think about the specific steps you took them through from beginning to end. Write down each step in detail. It's better to have too many steps at this stage than too few.

From there, you'll want to group steps together into phases that make sense, then think about changing the wording so that it resonates more with your clients. For example, if you work with doctors, maybe you want to use words like "diagnosis" and "prescribe" instead of "analyze" and "recommend." Taking the time to think about the details will help differentiate you and tell your niche your firm was designed for them.

Using my fictional company Aviation Capital Management, which serves commercial pilots, as an example, the proprietary process might look like this:

AVIATORS INCOME STABILIZER SYSTEM

Preflight: Analyze the current financial conditions and gather the necessary documents.

Flight Planning: Set your first financial goal and develop a plan. Insert data into your financial GPS.

In-Flight: Implement recommendations to navigate to your first goal. Conduct dead reckoning each month to see if you are on track.

Postflight: Beers at Hangar 24 are on us when you successfully land your first goal.

When the celebration is complete and enough time has passed "from bottle to throttle," we'll repeat the process and continue to be your copilot for each of your next financial goals.

This example is cheesy and over the top on purpose. I do this to clearly illustrate the point that your proprietary process can be more or less the same standard CFP Board process but described in language that is customized to your niche.

As you can tell, the process is still information gathering, goal setting, analysis and recommendation, implementation, and monitoring. You may not even understand my aviation references in this proprietary process because it wasn't designed for you! But every pilot would immediately understand my process and know it was designed for them.

CLIENT EXPERIENCE

Working with a niche will also give you the opportunity to create a unique client experience. The client experience includes your office, your staff, the deliverables you provide, and the technology you use.

My fictional company, Aviation Capital Management, has its office located above a hangar in a general aviation airport in San Diego's East County. Clients can taxi their planes right into the hangar for their appointments.

The CEO, Jackie Esperanza, recruits pilots who want to change careers to be associate advisors and then trains them to be full lead advisors in just a few years. Not only are these pilots-turned-advisors part of the niche community, but they also have a built-in network of potential clients. These new advisors have the capacity to bring in new clients from their very first day on the job.

Aviation Capital Management knows that today's pilots use sophisticated "electronic flight bags" on their iPads with continually updated information instead of static paper charts and flight information obtained by phone or computer. So, the financial planning software they offer clients has a mobile app optimized for tablets. Plans are updated in real time.

What can you do to make the client experience customized for your niche?

- **Office:** If your niche wants to come into an office, what physical changes would make it most comfortable for them (e.g., architecture, location, decor, meeting room layouts)?

- **Staff:** What staff members do you need to serve your clients? For example, can you recruit staff from your niche? Do you need certain specialists to serve your niche (e.g., an attorney on staff to review estate planning documents if you are in the legacy planning niche)?

- **Deliverables:** What deliverables does your niche want to see? Do they want a physical or electronic plan? Is there a creative way to present the deliverable?

- **Technology:** What technology will serve your niche best? Is there a client-facing software you want to offer? Do you need special software to help solve your clients' problems (e.g., business valuation software for the niche of business owners selling within five years)?

Remember Cathy Curtis, whom I introduced at the beginning of the book? After years of failing to differentiate herself, she eventually made a change that let her stay in the business she loves. She now specializes in self-made women in the San Francisco Bay Area.

On the recommendation of her peers, Cathy began implementing a financial life planning process with her clients, only to realize her niche just wasn't interested.

"My clients are get-down-to-brass-tacks types of ladies who

hire me to improve their financial lives, not to be their therapist," Cathy explains. "They are women who want a list of action items to achieve their already clearly envisioned goals. They want to implement what they already know is important to them . . . paying less in taxes, investing more in ESG, charitable giving, and retiring smart."

By understanding her niche, Cathy avoided implementing a popular financial planning process that her niche didn't want. And because she only works with one type of client, she can implement that same "get to the point" process for all of her clients.

Lindsey Swanson, in her work with legal sex workers, also adapts her client experience to match her clients' styles. "My clients will set a meeting with me, but their schedule will change, and they have to cancel. Or, because they are primarily in their twenties, they might be hungover or are working on three hours of sleep. In these cases, it might not be useful to have our monthly call. So, I send them a video answering any questions I know they have. That allows them to watch when it is best for them."

Lindsey explains, "We do all of our meetings virtual because my clients never know where they are going to be. For our meetings, they don't have to put on pants, and they can smoke or vape during our meetings. All of these things help them feel more comfortable with topics that are inherently uncomfortable."

By knowing their clients, these advisors were able to create a client experience that works for them instead of forcing them into an experience designed for people nothing like them.

SERVICES

Determining which services you offer may seem simple and not something that really needs much attention. After all, you will offer the same services as every other financial advisor firm: investment management, financial planning, retirement planning, tax planning, estate planning, and risk management.

But not all the services you currently offer may apply to your niche. Or there may be some services important to your niche you aren't currently offering. For example, if you work with business owners, you may need a service called Business Succession Planning.

Cathy Curtis discovered this in her work with self-made women in the San Francisco Bay Area. "As I worked more with these self-made women, I had to make tax planning a critical part of my business, which was not something I offered in the early years. I also incorporated ESG investments as an important part of my investment strategy since nearly every one of my clients is as much concerned about where their money is invested as maximizing the return of their investment."

As you are developing your service list, think about the wording that would impact your clients. For example, if you work with multigenerational firms, you may want to include "Family Legacy Planning" instead of estate planning. My fictional commercial pilot wouldn't be interested in estate planning because she would perceive that service as something only wealthy people need. But she would be aware that as a single person, she needs to make sure her money and insurance go to the right people in case of her death. So, Wills and Trust Review and Insurance Beneficiary Review may be the right service names for her.

Use this opportunity to customize your wording to be most impactful for your ideal client. But one warning: Don't get too creative to the point where your prospects won't understand what you are talking about. It should be clear to them what service you are offering without an explanation.

PRICING

Pricing is a sensitive subject in this industry. There are arguments about which is better, fee-only or fee-based. Should you charge AUM or hourly? I don't want to weigh in on the pricing debate other than to say your pricing should reflect what makes sense for your niche. For example, if you have a niche that is high earning but doesn't have investable assets, a traditional AUM fee model won't work unless you are willing to take a loss for several years, hoping they'll eventually have the assets to be profitable. Many firms who work with young physicians have this philosophy—they'll get them as clients while they are young, knowing they will be profitable clients over time.

If you want to get paid for your advice when you give it, you may need to develop a creative pricing model for your niche to be profitable. Here are a variety of scenarios where you need to be creative with your pricing because the AUM fees alone won't be sufficient for the service you provide:

- High-earning young professionals with no assets

- High-net-worth clients with little liquidity (e.g., business owners, real estate investors)

In addition, I have seen some niches that want to pay the advisor fees in a way that makes more sense to them:

- Attorneys who want to pay on a retainer

- Tech professionals who are willing to pay for tax and financial planning but like to manage their own investments using online trading platforms

To serve your niche, you may have to consider options outside of AUM, such as hourly, project-based, subscription, commission, flat fee, percentage of net worth, etc.

Eric Sigdestad focuses on the niche of employees of a Southern California telecommunications company. To build this niche, he had to get creative with his fees: "Because these employees have all of their wealth tied up in their company retirement plan, I meet with them once a year every year in the years leading up to retirement," he told me. "I have met with one client every year for the last seventeen years. But they usually become paying clients when they finally do retire."

There are a lot of advisors all competing for the same clients. Some advisors are lucky enough to work with a niche that has the assets and is willing to pay AUM fees. But other advisors will need to get creative with pricing. The key is to find the balance between the price the client is willing to pay for your value, and the fee that is profitable for you to offer your service.

Good niches may not immediately fall into a traditional AUM model and may require a creative (but still profitable) alternative fee structure. Ultimately, though, this can help keep the competition away (when they're all built around an AUM model that can't serve those clients). Though, to the extent the advisor focuses into a niche that builds wealth, it also generally will lead to AUM as well, in the future.

For example, a niche could focus on clients who are business owners selling their company to a family member. This niche has more complexity than most advisors want to touch until the sale of the business is done. This is because these types of sales often require unique financing structures, capital gains tax strategies, and maneuvering around complicated family and employee dynamics.

Advisory practices that focus on this niche may need a non-traditional fee model, as the client's assets are often tied up in the business (which hasn't yet had a liquidity event to turn into portfolio assets that can be managed) and other assets like real estate. Because advisors deserve to get paid what they are worth for their expertise and hard work to help clients make this transition, many advisors avoid this market altogether until a sale is imminent simply because the niche doesn't fit the popular AUM model. But if an advisor can structure their practice to help these business owners during their transition, they will have the cash to fit into an AUM model after the sale is complete.

Building a business model around your ideal client is the ultimate commitment to your niche. When you get to this stage, you want to be sure your niche is the right one for you. Clients who don't fit your niche will not fit well into your new business model, which means it will either be a disappointing experience for them or it will be incredibly hard, unprofitable work for you. Either way, it's likely to be a failure. But when you've found the right fit, it's a big win.

After niching on tech professionals, Bruce Barton was pleasantly surprised by how much it streamlined his operations. "It makes you think about how to do things better, cheaper, faster, with better outcomes for the client. These are things I didn't have the luxury to think about before. I was just spread too thin. Now I'm really targeted, and I think of ideas all the time for how to make my business better for my clients, my staff, and me."

Cathy Curtis had a similar experience. She recommends: "Turn down business that doesn't fit your niche as soon as you can. Only working with your niche makes everything easier. Your marketing is easier because you aren't tempted to try to please your outlier clients with content that appeals to them. You can build a service model thinking only about the needs of your ideal client and not worry about how to fit non-niche clients into it. You are able to streamline all aspects of your business operations."

When you get to this point, building a business model around the right niche is highly beneficial in multiple ways.

THE FINISHING PIECE TO THE UNCOMPARABLE FRAMEWORK

You might consider your proprietary business model as the capstone to your work as an uncomparable financial advisor with a niche practice. This business model will deepen your differentiation, build your credibility, and attract more prospective clients. It is also the final piece in understanding the Uncomparable Framework. Now it is time to start laying out the framework through tangible steps. You will use a three-year plan for this, which I explain in Part 3.

KEY TAKEAWAYS

- Uncomparable financial advisors design a proprietary business model specifically for their niche clients. Your business model will not come immediately but will instead evolve over time. In the beginning, you can adapt your existing structure to your niche.

- You want to customize your financial planning process to solve your niche's foremost problem. Having a custom process that speaks to your niche's needs will empower you, attract more clients, enable you to charge more, and make presentations easier and more effective.

- Your client experience should encompass your office, staff, deliverables, and technology. By knowing your niche, you can create a client experience suited to them.

- You may find that not all the services you offer apply to your niche. Or you may find that you need to add services. Regardless, you can be even more effective by adapting the language describing your services to resonate with your niche.

- Think outside of the box when it comes to pricing. Your niche may not fit the traditional AUM fee model yet still prove profitable. Your pricing should reflect what makes sense for you and your niche.

Part 3

THE PLAN

CHAPTER 9

The Three-Year Plan

Now that you understand the elements of the Uncomparable Framework, let's look at how you can implement it over roughly three years' time.

Why three years? In his article "Building a Niche Advisory Business: It Takes 3 Years for People to Know, Like, and Trust," Michael Kitces presents the idea that it "takes about 3 years for the exponential growth of a niche to really start to take off."[10]

That has also been my experience when working with financial advisors, as well as the estimation of many of the advisors I interviewed for this book.

Why does it take so long to build a niche advisory business? Kitces says that it takes "time to be known, liked, and trusted in the first place, especially as a financial advisor in our low-trust industry

---

10 Michael Kitces, "Building A Niche Advisory Business: It Takes 3 Years for People to Know, Like, and Trust," Kitces.com, August 4, 2014, https://www.kitces.com/blog/building-a-niche-advisory-business-it-takes-3-years-for-people-to-know-like-and-trust.

of financial services." But once you gain this trust and become the go-to person in a niche, your business takes off, and marketing becomes much easier.

Eric Sigdestad, the financial advisor who started his business niching to employees of a telecommunications company, summed it up this way: "Starting a niche is like getting a Boeing 747 jet to take off from LAX. It takes a lot of fuel for the 747 to taxi to the runway, get airborne, and then climb to cruising altitude. But once it finally gets to cruise altitude, the fuel burn rate is much more efficient. You have to invest a lot of time and money up front to get your niche to take off, but after that, the flight is smooth."

How fast you will grow depends on your current engagement with a niche. Kitces states that businesses that already have some connection to or presence within a niche can grow faster, while firms brand new to a niche will grow slower.

Three years may seem painfully long, but the investment will be worth it in the end. In reality, if you don't niche, you could easily spend the next three years throwing new tactics at the wall, making no progress. The time will go by anyway. If you niche, though, three years will go by quickly because you have a lot to do in that period.

The three-year plan I outline in Chapters 10, 11, and 12 is a similar formula I've seen work for solo practitioners just starting out, boutique RIAs, and multibillion-dollar AUM enterprise RIAs implementing a niche approach. The variations of tactics depend on the resources available, but the overall strategy is the same.

Before we look at what you should be working on in each of those three years, let's look at how you should think about the overall marketing strategy.

THINK ECOSYSTEM, NOT FUNNEL

When I ask financial advisors what their primary marketing goal is, one of the most common responses is, "I want to build a marketing funnel." If you aren't familiar with the term, a funnel lays out the steps to lead someone from a total lack of awareness about a product or service to the purchase of that product or service.

From a financial advisor's perspective, a marketing funnel is a theoretical path the prospective client takes from not knowing who you are, to gaining awareness, to researching you, to evaluating you, to finally becoming a client.

In consumer products, a funnel looks something like this: You, the consumer, see an ad for the company's candle on Facebook. You click the link, which takes you to a landing page selling that candle. Suddenly, a pop-up appears, offering you 15 percent off your first purchase if you give the company your email address. You do and then exit the website because you aren't ready to buy.

Now, three times a week, you get an email from this company promoting different candles. A month goes by, and you click the link to a landing page and buy a candle from them. This is the funnel: Facebook ad → landing page → pop-up form → promotional emails → landing page → purchase.

The idea behind funnels is that people don't make a purchase the first time they are introduced to a business. The company needs to nurture them before closing the sale.

Let's examine a funnel example for a financial advisor's business. You speak at an event. You encourage audience members to visit your website and provide their email addresses in exchange for a copy of the slides. Once they fill out the form, they get a series of automated emails recapping the presentation's key points and encouraging them to schedule an appointment. Then they schedule the appointment and become a client.

MARKETING FUNNEL

PRESENTATION

↓

LANDING PAGE WITH SLIDES

↓

DRIP EMAILS

↓

CALENDAR

↓

SIGNED AGREEMENT

Sounds great, right? The problem is that marketing rarely works like this when you offer a high-priced, high-commitment service. Prospects don't follow this neat theoretical funnel. It's common to nurture relationships for years and have dozens of touchpoints from all different channels.

It's usually not until the prospect has a painful and urgent financial matter they need you to solve that they hire you. The purchasing process is not linear. It looks more like an interconnected network of marketing activities—an ecosystem.

A more realistic scenario is that the prospect sees you speak at an event, and they download your slides, ignore your drip emails completely, and receive your monthly newsletter (which they also ignore). But they see your name month after month.

Two years in, they are on a social media group you also belong to, and they see your comment answering a financial question that's been on their mind. The next time they get your newsletter, they decide to open it just to see what you are up to. They notice you are hosting a webinar on a topic that has been concerning them lately, and they attend the webinar. Dropping into a new set of drip emails, they also ignore these. But they decide to connect with you on their favorite social media site and see your updates weekly while still getting your newsletter.

A year later, some sort of money-in-motion event common for their niche happens (e.g., being laid off, a spouse dying, selling an appreciated asset). All of a sudden, they need financial help. And you are the first person who comes to mind. Finally, they schedule the appointment, go through your sales process, and become a client.

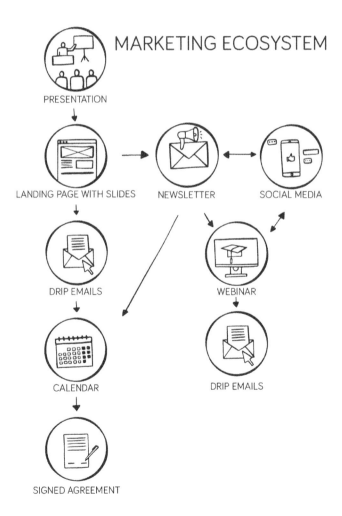

MARKETING ECOSYSTEM

PRESENTATION

LANDING PAGE WITH SLIDES   NEWSLETTER   SOCIAL MEDIA

DRIP EMAILS   WEBINAR

CALENDAR   DRIP EMAILS

SIGNED AGREEMENT

It takes time and effort to gain the trust needed for your prospects to hand over their life savings to you. And because it's a relationship that usually lasts their lifetime, it's a huge commitment on their part to work with you. Expecting people to trust and hire you simply because they have been funneled into your marketing process is unrealistic.

Hourly planning or commission-based services may have more success with a traditional marketing funnel because the perceived costs and commitment are low. But when you offer a service that may end up costing north of two hundred thousand dollars over a client's lifetime, funnels don't work as many would have you believe. You are not just asking them to hand over twenty-five dollars for a candle. You are asking them to trust you with their net worth.

Trust has to be built, and you do this through a marketing ecosystem like the one described here. Funnels do have value. Each campaign you implement should be designed using a funnel framework. It provides one hypothetical path for prospects to follow to become a client. While they probably won't follow the funnel, the structure helps shore up any holes in your process.

Your overall marketing strategy, though, should comprise a network of interconnecting and interacting parts. It should be an ecosystem. Now that you know how your marketing strategy will conceptually look, let's get to creating your plan.

SETTING GOALS

The first step in creating any plan is to set goals. But before we start, let's talk about two types of goals that will be used to guide your behavior and decision-making: outcome goals and activity goals. Outcome goals are focused on the results or outcomes that you want to achieve, such as losing ten pounds, acquiring twenty-five new clients, or achieving five million dollars in revenue. Activity goals are focused on the actions or behaviors that you need to take in order to achieve your outcome goals. Examples include restricting calorie intake to fifteen hundred per day or scheduling meetings with ten COIs each month.

Outcome goals provide a clear and motivating target to work toward, and they can help you to measure your progress and determine whether you have achieved your desired results. However, outcome goals can also be difficult to control, as they often depend on factors outside of your control.

Activity goals, on the other hand, are more focused on the actions that you can take to move closer to your outcome goals. They can help you to break down your goals into smaller, more manageable steps, and they can provide a sense of accomplishment and progress as you complete each step. Activity goals can also be easier to control, as you have more control over your own actions and behaviors.

Ultimately, you will want to set a combination of outcome goals (to set the vision) and activity goals (to set the activities) to achieve your desired outcomes.

In the first year, it can be challenging to set outcome-based goals for your niche, such as revenue, AUM, or new client goals, since you don't have enough information to accurately predict that yet. You also don't know whether you will accomplish them or not until the end. And then the result is either you win or you lose (did you lose those ten pounds or not?). They aren't the most motivating goals when you are starting with a niche.

However, you still want an outcome goal to serve as the visual destination for where you are heading. Set these goals based on what you would ideally like to achieve, but still, be realistic. But don't beat yourself up if you don't achieve them. Growth can be slow in the first years, with an exponential increase starting after year three.

In your first few years, focus on activity-based goals that you can control on a daily and weekly basis. What gets measured gets done—these goals are easily trackable, and you can see when you are getting off course. When this happens, you can easily get back on track the next day without judgment. For example, if you your activity goal is to restrict your daily calorie intake to 1,500 calories, but you splurge one day and have 2,500 calories, you can easily get back on track the next day.

With activity-based goals, you can see whether that activity is generating results you are satisfied with or not and then determine if you need to increase your activity or try a different approach. It's a learning system that allows you to constantly pivot and improve. What are some examples of activity-based goals?

- Schedule meetings with ten influencers in my niche each month

- Write one blog every week and submit it to XYZ publication as a guest post

- Spend thirty minutes each weekday connecting and interacting with my niche on social media

How do you determine which activities you should be doing? I'll go into more detail on ideas for each year in Chapters 10, 11, and 12. But first, let's discuss developing a marketing plan.

CREATE QUARTERLY MARKETING PLANS

When you determine your marketing activities, you will need to hold yourself and your team accountable for implementing them. I recommend you do this with a written marketing plan. A marketing plan serves the important function of identifying specific activities that need to be accomplished, including deadlines and assigning someone to be accountable.

You may think you need to create an annual marketing plan, but in the book *The 12 Week Year: Get More Done in 12 Weeks Than Others Do in 12 Months*, author Brian Moran proposes a different way to create a plan—by shortening your planning period from one year to twelve weeks.[11]

The argument is that if you develop a twelve-week plan, every task in your plan will be actionable. With only twelve weeks to implement the plan, you have a built-in sense of urgency that doesn't allow for procrastination. A twelve-week plan also means you are more likely to complete the action items you commit to, making it more feasible to hit your goals.

The problem is that, like a financial plan, a static annual marketing plan becomes outdated quickly because the business environment is constantly changing. For example, I have seen marketing plans change quickly because of monumental events such as the Great Recession in 2008 and the COVID-19 pandemic in 2020. Most annual marketing plans developed in the months leading up to these events had to be adjusted to match the new world reality. While a drastic shift in strategy like that required during the Great Recession or the COVID-19 pandemic is rare, having to adapt marketing tactics based on new opportunities and threats is not. A year is simply too long to accurately predict what tactics will be required to work toward your strategy.

---

11 Brian F. Moran and Michael Lennington, *The 12 Week Year: Get More Done in 12 Weeks Than Others Do in 12 Months* (New York: Wiley, 2013).

Besides becoming irrelevant quickly, annual marketing plans face other issues:

- The twelve-month timeline is so long it becomes tempting to procrastinate and put off tasks for another day, month, or quarter.

- An annual plan can't foresee all the things you will learn as you implement various tactics. Your experience and results may significantly change your strategy and tactics.

- A twelve-month plan doesn't anticipate the opportunities that will arise as you succeed in implementing your plan (e.g., speaking engagements pop up, you get invited to be a podcast guest).

- It is not designed to adapt, so when tactics become outdated, the entire marketing plan gets disregarded.

Because some of your marketing activities will occur weekly (e.g., blogs, videos, podcasts), I find it's easier to plan for a full thirteen-week quarter than the twelve-week period Moran suggests. Here's how to create a detailed marketing plan for thirteen weeks:

Step 1: Establish Your Overall Objectives for Your Marketing for the Quarter

What would you like to accomplish for the quarter? In Chapters 10, 11, and 12, I will give you the specific areas of marketing focus for each of the first three years of launching your niche. You should pull from this list. If you finish one year early, start pulling from the next year.

Be realistic on what you can accomplish. It is better to focus on just a few things you can finish than to start many things without finishing them. Do not include "parking lot ideas" that you would like to get to someday. They will only distract you from the activities that will make a difference.

Step 2: Break Down Tasks

Using a spreadsheet, use one column to record all the tasks needed to maintain your existing marketing—for example, send a monthly newsletter, meet with ten influencers, record six podcast episodes. If you just started your niche, you probably won't have many, if any, of these maintenance tasks. In the same column, write down all the tasks required to implement the objectives you identified in Step 1 above.

You may find that the number of tasks required to implement all your objectives is not feasible in one quarter. If this is the case, adjust by picking just one or two objectives to focus on.

Here are examples of tasks:

- Write blog on [topic]

- Promote blog on social media

- Contact [center of influence name] to schedule lunch

- Attend lunch with [center of influence name]

- Ask [client name] to make an introduction to [name] at [organization]

- Send monthly newsletter

- Send invitation for webinar

- Research search engine optimization companies

- Choose website developer from companies interviewed

Step 3: Assign Each Task to a Week

In a second column, assign a week (1-13) to each of the tasks in the first column. I recommend you include the date of the first day of the week to make visualization easier—for example, "Week 1: April 4."

You will need to put tasks in the order you need to accomplish them. For example, if you want to launch a new website, the tasks might be:

- Research website companies (Week 1)

- Schedule appointments with website companies (Week 2)

- Meet with ABC website company (Week 3)

- Meet with DEF website company (Week 3)

- Meet with XYZ website company (Week 4)

- Decide which company to hire (Week 6)

You may not have the information you need during your planning session to include all the required tasks, but you can add new tasks later. In the example above, you will add your tasks to meet with specific website companies to the correct week once you schedule the appointments. You will add the tasks for website development once you know the process and timeline for the company you hire.

If you find you have too many tasks after assigning them to specific weeks, you may have to make cuts. The quarterly marketing plan is designed to keep you accountable and stop procrastination. If you know you won't be able to accomplish all the tasks, create a more realistic plan.

■	TASK	DATE	ACC
WEEK 1			
☐			
☐			
☐			

Step 4: Execute and Track

With your quarterly plan in place, all you have to do now is follow the plan and execute the tasks assigned to each week. If something new comes up that needs to be integrated into your plan (e.g., speak at ABC accounting firm), add the task to the correct week. This is not an invitation to add new "shiny object" distractions to your plan. Instead, consider new opportunities resulting from your efforts.

At the end of each week, mark each task as "complete" or "not complete." If a task is partially complete, record it as "not complete" because you did not accomplish it by the date you set for yourself. You can then copy and paste the task into another row and assign it to the week you plan on completing it.

If you have weekly company meetings, I suggest that you report what the company has accomplished the prior week and what will be accomplished the current week in order to provide further accountability.

Step 5: Analyze and Plan

At the end of each quarter, review the results from your current quarter and plan for the next one.

Did you take on too much, and do you need to adjust expectations next quarter? Do you need to free up time or hire additional help to implement? Conversely, can you take on more next quarter and make even faster progress toward your marketing objectives? And, no matter how well you implemented your plan, where is there room for improvement next quarter?

Once you have analyzed your completed quarterly marketing plan, repeat Steps 1-5 for the next quarter.

With the shorter thirteen-week time frame, you can adapt your strategies as needed and accomplish more. The end result? A better marketing system for you and your firm.

TRACK YOUR MARKETING

As soon as you start implementing your first quarterly marketing plan, start tracking information about your prospects. Tracking this information will not only help you track your success but will also help inform future decisions about which marketing to do going forward. Collecting data from the beginning will help you observe trends and measure the results of your marketing.

There is only one marketing metric that ultimately matters—how many qualified prospects scheduled an appointment. And there is only one sales metric that matters—how many prospects became clients. Other metrics such as website visitors, social media followers, or email subscribers can serve as data points to help guide future sales and marketing decisions. But they do not measure success or failure on their own.

Let's say you host two different events. One event had thirty people attend. One event had three people attend. Which one was the success? You probably would say the event with thirty people was a success, and the one with three was a failure. But what if I said 33.3 percent from the first event and 66.7 percent from the second event scheduled appointments? You would probably say the second event was more successful. What if I said five people became clients from the first event, and one person became a client from the second event? In that case, you would probably say the first event was more successful. Finally, what if I told you that the first event produced $2.5 million in assets, but the second event produced $8 million in assets? You would then say the second event was more successful.

Focus on appointments and clients. Everything else is just data to guide your marketing hypotheses.

Use a CRM like Salesforce or a spreadsheet to track this information about your prospects:

- Name

- First Contact Date (the date they reached out to schedule an appointment)

- Meeting Date (first meeting date)

- Lead Source (e.g., client referral, COI referral, website, Google search, LinkedIn)

- Stage in the Sales Pipeline (e.g., initial contact, appointment scheduled, follow-up, closed—lost, closed—not a fit, closed—won)

- Assets/Revenue (pick the one you primarily measure)

- Closed Date (the date they became a client)

You may decide you want to track more information like who referred them or why they reached out, but this list is a good starting point.

By tracking this information, you will be able to analyze these factors:

- Number of prospects per lead source

- Number of clients per lead source

- Number of new prospects per month and per year

- New assets/revenue per month and per year

- New assets/revenue per lead source

- Stages where prospects are getting stuck in or falling off the sales cycle

- Sales cycle—the average time from initial contact to signing contracts

- Close rate—the number of new clients closed divided by the total number of prospects who set appointments

With this information, you can make tweaks to your sales and marketing or reallocate resources to more successful marketing channels.

DON'T OBSESS ABOUT VANITY METRICS

I often see advisors obsess over marketing metrics such as website visitors and social media followers—in other words, "vanity metrics." These numbers make you feel good, but they aren't leading indicators of whether you are becoming uncomparable or of your business's future success. For example, if you are measuring traffic to your website, you may assume that an increase in traffic may signal that you should be getting more appointments set. But all it really means is that there is some content on the website that is ranking high in the search engines. That doesn't necessarily mean that content will convert to appointments, and if it does convert to appointments, it doesn't mean prospects are qualified.

Instead, you want to focus your analysis on metrics that truly help inform your strategy:

- Number of people who scheduled appointments

- Lead source (e.g., website, referral) of new prospects

- Conversion rate

These types of metrics will tell you what you are doing right and where you have room to improve.

HOW YOUR OVERALL STRATEGY BREAKS DOWN

Now that you have an idea of how your overall strategy will be structured and how to develop a plan, you may be asking yourself, what activities should I be focusing on? In Chapters 10, 11, and 12, I will give you a breakdown of the activities you should focus on each year over the first three years of your niche.

KEY TAKEAWAYS

- It's unrealistic to think the traditional marketing funnel will work as an overall strategy. New clients must entrust their money and time to you, so it stands to reason that you will need to nurture prospects over years. Think of your strategy as an ecosystem of interdependent parts, building a prospect's trust over time.

- Initially, you cannot accurately predict outcome-based goals. Instead, create activity-based goals. After a few years, you will have a basis for outcome-based goals, but you should still focus on measurable activities.

- The traditional annual marketing plan can get outdated quickly and invites procrastination. Instead, create a thirteen-week quarterly plan that includes establishing objectives, breaking down tasks, assigning each one to a week, executing and tracking, and analyzing and planning for the next quarterly plan.

- With the Uncomparable Framework, you are freed from fretting over website visitors, social media followers, and other vanity metrics. Instead, you want to track information about your prospects so you can observe trends and measure marketing results.

CHAPTER 10

Year One

You are now ready to start planning your first year of launching your niche. The first year of building a niche business that makes you uncomparable should be spent creating a marketing foundation—solidifying your message, establishing your expertise, and networking with everyone you can in your niche. It also means doing everything you can to build your database so you can start the nurturing clock with your network as soon as possible. In this chapter, I cover the specific steps you should take in your first year.

As these steps span across the framework, some of this will be reiterating earlier points, but I'd like to touch in again at the level of depth that is appropriate for each year. Most of these recommendations apply to the solo practitioner, the employee advisor, the boutique RIA, and the enterprise RIA. In some cases, I have included variations if the recommendation differs based on the advisor or firm type.

NICHE: DEFINE YOUR NICHE

This step may seem obvious, but it is critical to get clear on whom you serve. Unless you are an enterprise RIA implementing a multi-niche approach, the more specific the niche, the better. Instead of using the broad category of "executives," niche down to "director-level and higher in the STEM field with equity compensation issues." This narrow focus will serve most individual advisors and boutique firms better in the long run.

POSITION: CRAFT YOUR MESSAGE

Develop a clear and specific message that resonates with your niche. Identify the one problem your niche shares, then communicate how you solve that problem for them and what the successful outcome looks like. This message needs to be simple and consistently communicated on your website and in your elevator pitch, marketing materials, online profiles, and every marketing piece you create. The one caveat here is that enterprise RIAs implementing a multi-niche approach may decide to downplay the niche messaging in their company-wide marketing assets like company social media profiles.

POSITION: ESTABLISH YOUR VISUAL BRAND

With a clear niche and message, develop or update your brand to appeal to the people in your niche. This does not mean you have to invest a lot of time or money in developing an incredibly unique brand. It means you need to use colors and images that appeal to your niche. For example, does your niche prefer to see images of multigenerational families or supermodel-looking people on private jets? Do they prefer soothing colors like blue or elegant colors like gold?

If you own or are an employee of an enterprise RIA, you won't be able to change your existing brand. However, consider switching out pictures on your niche webpage and other niche-focused marketing materials to reflect your niche client. If you are a boutique RIA and haven't decided you aren't going all in on your niche yet, follow these same instructions.

In general, don't get distracted focusing on your brand at this stage. Do enough to appeal to and not repel your prospective clients. You should only focus your entire company brand on your niche when you are starting a business from scratch or you are 100 percent confident in your future success with your niche.

POSITION: BUILD A LANDING PAGE OR WEBSITE

Once you have your brand and your message, the next step is to update your website. Whether you dedicate just one page or an entire site to your niche, it will serve as the hub for your future marketing efforts. It will also house all content that positions you as an expert. Finally, it provides a way for people to schedule appointments with you.

If you have an existing business in place and have been serving clients for several years, create a separate web page dedicated to your niche on your existing website. You don't want to alienate your existing clients at this time by changing your homepage to be completely focused on your new niche. Start with just one page and include a link in your main navigation.

If you are a solo practitioner just starting out and are ready to go all in from the start, then develop your entire site to your niche. You don't have much to lose, and in fact, this focus and dedication will actually help you get clients faster.

In some cases, you will need to build a completely separate website (though I would avoid this whenever possible). You would do this if your niche is substantially different from your existing client base. You may also do this if you are an employee advisor and the firm does not want your niche associated with the wider brand. If this last scenario is you, speak to your company before going rogue and implementing this on your own since it may be a compliance violation.

NETWORK: CONDUCT INFORMATIONAL INTERVIEWS

Once you have your foundation, it is now time to spread the word about your niche. The fastest way to get in front of your niche is to announce it through your existing client and center of influence relationships that are already integrated into the niche community.

I recommend taking an "informational interview" approach commonly used by new college graduates exploring career options. With this approach, you ask people to meet with you one-on-one to get their feedback on your new service. You are honoring them by asking them for their opinion and expertise while planting the seed for introductions and referrals. This approach is effective for four reasons:

1. It allows you to announce your new service to key stakeholders without coming across as salesy.

2. It provides you with valuable feedback on your message and service that you can use to make your offering even more impactful.

3. Involving these stakeholders in the process creates a connection to your service. If they contribute to the development, they are more likely going to want to help you succeed.

4. You are planting the seed for future introductions and referrals.

As you begin to announce your service, start with your clients who also fall into your niche. Your clients have the most experience with you and the solutions you offer, and this will provide you with insight you may not have thought of. In addition, because there is already a trusted relationship established, they may be eager to provide you with a warm introduction to the niche community.

Next, reach out to centers of influence whom you have strong relationships with. Centers of influence may have insight into your niche market that you might not have thought of. The right COIs may already have relationships with your niche and can eventually provide introductions to their clients in the future. Involving them in the process helps create a connection to your service and plants a seed for future referrals.

During your conversation with both your clients and COIs, ask what challenges the niche faces and why they need a specialist. You should also ask them where you might be able to find other niche clients to give you future marketing ideas.

The benefit of starting with informational interviews with people you know is that it minimizes the impact of any missteps you might make along the way. For example, maybe you learn from an existing client that certain terminology doesn't resonate with the niche. You may use the word holistic to indicate a whole-picture approach to the financial planning you do for doctors, but one of your clients tells you that some doctors will have a negative association with the word depending on their opinions on holistic medicine. With this feedback, you avoid making that mistake before you announce your service to a larger audience.

I recommend conducting at least ten informational interviews in your first quarterly marketing plan. These conversations will help uncover opportunities and give you some much-needed momentum.

NETWORK: REENGAGE LOST PROSPECTS

A new niche-specific service is a perfect excuse to reengage lost prospects who fit your niche if you have an existing business. These may be current people in your pipeline, or they may be past lost prospects. This tactic will be easier for existing businesses that already have some experience with the niche.

Announcing your new services to prospects requires a different strategy than the informational interview you use with clients and COIs. Because they are worried about being "sold," they generally aren't going to be interested in helping you out. The strategy here is to tell them how you can help them. Let them know what's in it for them. You do this by personally reaching out and letting them know that you have a new service that was designed to solve the financial challenges of people just like them. In this step, you probably won't get much feedback as to ways to improve your message and offering, but it can help you determine if there's interest within your niche and give you some quick wins by booking a few appointments.

NETWORK: ANNOUNCE YOUR NICHE

After you've talked to COIs, clients, and prospects, you will be ready to create a general one-to-many announcement for all your contacts, telling them about your new specialization working with your niche. This is an optional step. If you are not fully committed to your niche yet, you can skip it for now. If you are ready, send out an email blast to your entire email list and promote the announcement on your personal and company social media profiles.

EXPERTISE: BLOG

You need to position yourself as an expert as quickly as possible. I find the best way to do this is through a blog. Not only does writing force you to learn what you need to know to be an expert in a niche, but it's also the best way to showcase the expertise you are learning.

Having this content on your website gives you credibility with anyone researching you online. You can also submit blogs to other publications or websites as guest posts to help get you in front of more people. Finally, if optimized for search engines, blogs can drive significant traffic to your website.

If you are juggling an existing business, write two blogs per month. See if you can get multiple advisors in your firm to contribute content to lessen the load. Or consider a ghostwriter or AI to assist in your efforts. If you are starting out a brand-new business with a niche, then weekly is the recommended frequency.

EXPERTISE: VIDEO BLOGS

If blogging is not your thing, you can substitute it for video blogs. Create videos addressing the same topics you would for blogs. Have the videos transcribed and put them on your website for additional content. You do not need to do both blogs and video blogs in your first year. Choose one format in year one and add on other formats in future years. Again, I would recommend a minimum of two per month, but more frequently is better.

COMMUNITY: NETWORK, NETWORK, NETWORK

I can't emphasize this enough. In the first year, meet as many people in your niche as possible. One method is through information interviews that have already been addressed. This is a must for everyone reading this book, though it may vary between in-person interviews or Zoom meetings depending on your niche.

A second method is through attending in-person networking events. This is mostly required for advisors who don't already have an established niche network—usually employee advisors or new solo practitioners. If there is a live event your niche is attending, be there! If you have an established boutique RIA or an enterprise RIA, you probably have a large enough network you can forgo this and focus on networking with your existing relationships.

A third method is through online networking. This means joining online groups and interacting with the members. Because this is a time-consuming activity, I find this is better for employee advisors or new solo advisors without preexisting networks to help spread the word.

Marlon Wesh snuck his way into a Facebook group with fifty thousand traveling nurses. He scoured through the posts searching for the financial problems they were talking about.

"I searched for specific terms like *taxes*, *retirement*, and *investing*. And from that, I would see what questions the nurses were asking one another. I would then record a video answering the question, go back to the Facebook post, and reply with, 'Hey, I recorded this video a while ago about this topic. Hope it's interesting. I think it might answer your question.'"

This approach allowed Marlon to network daily with a niche he would have a hard time reaching through live events.

NETWORK: BUILD YOUR DATABASE

Networking in the early days of your niche strategy will accelerate the timeline for results. When you are doing your informational interviews with clients and COIs, ask them for introductions to other people in the niche—not for referral purposes, but just to expand your network. And then add all those people to your marketing database (i.e., your email marketing system).

Every time you meet a new person associated with your niche, connect with them on the appropriate social media site (if you aren't sure, just connect on LinkedIn) and add them to your marketing list. The goal is to meet as many people as possible and build your database of leads and centers of influence as quickly as you can.

For enterprise RIAs implementing a multi-niche approach, you can usually accomplish this by sorting through your existing database of clients and centers of influence and tagging them as someone in one of your niches. You can include them in all future marketing activities directed to that niche.

Rules regarding adding people to your email list vary by state and country and are getting stricter by the day. Check regulations prior to sending mass, unsolicited emails (i.e., your newsletter).

NETWORK: NURTURE YOUR NETWORK

Staying top of mind with your niche community will yield enormous benefits in future years. To stay top of mind, create an email newsletter featuring content (usually pulled from your blog) specific to your niche. Continuously build your database of every contact, prospect, client, and influencer who belongs to your niche community, and send the newsletter at least once a month. In the beginning, if you can send a weekly newsletter, do it. You need to get your name out there.

Connect with everyone you meet on social media. To stay top of mind, post not only the content you create but share other niche-relevant content that you curate from other sources. You want your name coming up in their social media feeds often enough that they remember your name. You can use social media scheduling software to post on your behalf, and you can reuse content by changing the description of the post. If you are a new solo practitioner or solo advisor, I recommend spending thirty minutes a day interacting with your niche on social media. I have found this to be an unrealistic expectation for established firms, in which case I recommend just posting original content a few times per week, depending on the site.

EXPERTISE: PRESENT TO GROUPS

In case I haven't repeated myself enough, year one is about getting in front of as many people as possible. While one option is to do this one person at a time, it is more efficient to get in front of groups of many people at once. Find as many groups as you can to present to during your first year in a niche. Not only will this help you reach multiple people at once but it will also open up more speaking opportunities in the future.

Develop *one* presentation that addresses your niche's primary financial concern and gives them the steps to solving their problem or achieving their goal. This presentation should mimic the steps you take to solve this problem when working with a client. This helps presell your prospects when they schedule an appointment. Use this same presentation for the entire year, making tweaks along the way and altering to meet the time requirements.

It can be easy to commit to developing different presentations for each group you speak to, but this presents two problems. The first is that you just don't have the time to create presentations for each group. The second problem is that when you change up your presentation, you aren't reinforcing your message. And repetition is key to getting the word out about what you're doing.

The groups you speak to don't have to be formal. You can start by presenting to a handful of clients you already work with, or maybe you just present to friends who fit your niche. Smaller groups are better in the beginning because they allow you time to work through and perfect your material.

If you are an enterprise RIA, you probably have enough clients in your niche that you can start hosting client events and ask your clients to invite guests.

Collect the contact information, including the email address, of everyone who attends your presentation and add them to your database for future nurturing campaigns.

Educational events are generally preferred to social events, though I've seen both work well. With a social event, you will usually get more people to attend, but they may not be in the mindset of wanting to work with you. With an educational event, you will probably attract fewer people, but the attendees are likely to have the pain point you are addressing and will hear your message.

When you have a presentation ready, you can take advantage of last-minute speaking opportunities. You can also repurpose it into fifteen or thirty minutes and put it on your website as an on-demand webinar that can serve as a lead magnet.

COMMUNITY: ADD YOUR NAME TO DIRECTORIES

Adding your name to online directories is usually an inexpensive way to passively market your business. These can be financial advisor-specific directories like NAPFA's Find an Advisor. But the majority of these sites are location specific (e.g., thirty miles from Kansas City), which will not work for advisors focused on a national niche. Use these sites if your niche is local, such as business owners or widows.

There will also be niche-specific directories you can utilize. For example, if you are niching in eldercare, there are many nonprofit association websites that link to resources associated with caring for the elderly.

Finally, you can list yourself on general business directory sites like Yelp or Nextdoor. These are generally localized, though, so they don't work well for those in a national niche.

Pay for the directories that would pay for themselves if they produced just one client. I generally recommend avoiding the sites that charge by the lead or charge a percentage of revenue. These are sites generalists would use, not uncomparable advisors.

EXPERTISE: DEVELOP A LEAD MAGNET

As you spread the word about what you are doing, you'll generate more interest in your business and drive more traffic to your website. Since not all those who are curious about you will be ready to do business, you'll want a way to capture their names and email addresses so you can nurture the relationship until they are ready to schedule an appointment.

The simplest way to do this is through a PDF resource like an eBook or checklist. You can also consider an on-demand webinar using the same presentation you are using to present to groups. The important thing is that the resource is something your niche will value, that it addresses their primary pain point and gives them a solution mimicking how you would help them if they were a client, and that you offer it in exchange for their email address.

In the first year, only create one lead magnet. You don't need to waste energy creating multiple pieces. You can expand in future years, though I have seen some firms successfully stick to just one lead magnet for years at a time.

COMMUNITY: RESPOND TO MEDIA REQUESTS

Sign up for a media request list such as those common with organizations like NAPFA or HelpAReporter.com (HARO). When you receive inquiries, only respond to the ones that are specific and relevant to your niche. While being quoted in these publications is unlikely to turn into new business, they will help add to your credibility, open you up to new opportunities to be quoted, provide more content for you to share on social media, and improve your website's search engine optimization. Because this is a time-consuming tactic, this is usually recommended for new solo practitioners who are not inundated with client work. For more established firms, this is something that can be delegated to an administrative professional to review and bring you just the best opportunities worth pursuing.

BUSINESS MODEL: SET YOUR PRICING

To get your first niche clients to work with you, you may have to address your pricing model. This is mostly true if you charge on the traditional AUM fee structure, and your niche does not fit. Your pricing should reflect what makes sense for your niche. If you want to get paid for your advice when you give it, you may need to develop a creative pricing model for your niche to be profitable.

You may have to consider options outside of AUM, such as hourly, project-based, subscription, commission, flat fee, and percentage of net worth. This gets significantly more difficult or even impossible to implement for enterprise RIAs or well-established boutique RIAs traditionally charging AUM fees. And employee advisors are likely to have no possibility of doing this. If that's your situation, hopefully you chose a niche that fits an AUM model.

BUSINESS MODEL: CUSTOMIZE SERVICES

There may be some services important to your niche that fall outside of comprehensive financial planning (e.g., investment management, financial planning, retirement planning, tax planning, estate planning, and risk management) that your niche needs. For example, if you work with business owners, you may need to provide business succession planning.

Even if you don't plan on adding new services, customize how you describe your current services to be most meaningful for your ideal client. For example, if you work with multigenerational families, you may want to describe "estate planning" as "family legacy planning" instead.

ONE STEP AT A TIME

If you feel overwhelmed by what lies ahead of you, you can feel better by creating your activities-based marketing plan. By translating your first year's implementation into quarterly activities, you will find that the organization makes the process feel much more doable—just as your clients feel after they see their financial plan!

Your first year is about getting yourself known. In the second year, which I cover in Chapter 11, you build on your efforts by expanding your reach.

KEY TAKEAWAYS

- Your first year of a niche marketing strategy is pivotal. Use this year to solidify your message, establish expertise, and build and nurture your network.

- You start by defining your niche and positioning yourself as their expert for guidance. Then craft your message, establish a visual brand, and create a landing page or website for your niche.

- Establish your expertise via blogs, videos, presentations, and lead magnets. And reach your niche by networking with anyone and everyone in the community.

- As you establish yourself in your community, you build your network. Talk to COIs, clients, and prospects about your niche and fine-tune your messaging based on their feedback. Once you have done this, announce your niche publicly.

- Finally, work on your business model by establishing your pricing and customizing your services to attract your niche.

CHAPTER 11

Year Two

In year two, your efforts get more sophisticated as you expand your reach through new channels. You will offer more frequent or more in-depth content, look for opportunities to be a guest speaker, expand into advertising, and take your process to a niche-specific level.

Let's look at what you need to do in year two.

COMMUNITY: GUEST EVERYWHERE

You should continue to focus on getting in front of your niche as much as possible. By year two, you should have established enough credibility to be able to contribute your thoughts to various media outlets. Look for opportunities to be a guest speaker at live or virtual events, be a guest on podcasts, and contribute guest articles to websites and publications.

I worked with an employee advisor who has a specialty in working with real estate professionals. Each month, he submits at least one guest post to real estate agent magazines or websites. His first success from this strategy resulted in gaining a high-net-worth real estate agent located two states away from his primary geographic market.

When you have an opportunity to leverage someone else's network, you take it, no matter how insignificant. These opportunities not only build your credibility but also lead to additional opportunities.

EXPERTISE: EXPAND AND REPURPOSE YOUR CONTENT

Once you are in the habit of consistently creating blogs (or video blogs), you can expand your content. If you like to write, you can continue to write blogs but add longer, more in-depth content. If that is not an option, increase the number of blogs you write each month (say from two to four). You can also develop videos to enhance your blogs or to share on their own. Or you can start designing interesting infographics for your niche.

You will also have enough content to start repurposing it. Cut longer videos into shorter snippets to share on social media. Reverse blog topics you've written from the positive to the negative or vice versa (e.g., "Ten Tips to Sell Your Business" to "Ten Mistakes to Avoid When Selling Your Business") and share them in new places. Record your podcast interviews as a video and share them on YouTube. Repurposing content is something you can easily outsource to a freelancer or marketing agency if you want to save time.

EXPERTISE: OPTIMIZE CONTENT FOR SEARCH ENGINES

If you consistently write blogs in year one on topics your niche truly cares about, your website will likely start to rank for some keywords your niche is searching for. In year two, start making more deliberate efforts to optimize your content and overall website to drive more search traffic.

When people have questions, the first place they usually look for an answer is on the internet, whether that is through searching on Google or YouTube. The key to using search to your benefit is to identify the most pressing questions prospects who would be interested in your services may search for. You then develop content that provides them with an answer.

This content creation is the first step. The second step is to optimize your content so that your prospect is likely to find it on Google or another search engine (or YouTube if you produce videos).

Search engine optimization is a pretty technical concept and is constantly changing, so you would be well served to hire a company to help you with your SEO efforts. Your time should be spent proactively getting in front of your niche, not learning the latest technique (which will change before you've had a chance to master it) to drive traffic to your website.

Investing in a search engine optimization strategy doesn't necessarily get you in front of your target market as quickly as other strategies, but it can provide compounded rewards over the long run in the form of new prospects.

NETWORK: DEVELOP A COI NURTURING SYSTEM

In your first year, you talk to anyone you can think of associated with your niche. In year two, it's time to implement a deliberate and systematized effort to meet new centers of influence and nurture those relationships for referrals.

If you don't have a large existing COI network, you'll need to focus on networking to build one. Research networking events to attend to meet new COIs you can add to your professional network. Add these networking events to your quarterly marketing calendar and hold yourself accountable to attend. This tactic is appropriate for solo practitioners and employee advisors.

No matter the size of your firm or your status, decide which methods you would like to use and how often you want to keep in touch with your COIs. This can be mass touchpoints like a newsletter, group events like a hospitality suite at a sporting event, or one-on-one interactions like coffee or a round of golf. Your budget and the size of your network will determine these touchpoints. Schedule each of those touchpoints into your marketing plan.

It can take years of relationship-building to gain the trust required for COIs to provide a referral. Starting these efforts in year two will pay dividends in future years.

NETWORK: DEVELOP A LEAD NURTURING SYSTEM

Over year one, you have aggressively built your marketing database and used your newsletter to keep in touch with your prospects. Because it can take someone several years to finally take action on their finances and schedule an appointment, your lead database is your richest source of new clients. It's time to tap into that asset and add another layer to nurture these leads.

Kristin Harad, a marketing consultant who helps financial advisors build and improve campaign funnels, divides lead nurturing into two categories. "First, look at how to communicate to your entire database on a calendar basis on topics that affect everyone in your niche. For example, you could send a year-end tax planning video in early November to your entire list. Second, look at how to nurture your leads one-on-one, depending on where they are in their relationship with you. For example, is this person opening every newsletter and regularly clicking on articles? If so, they are interested and engaged, and it might be time for a personal email from you."

While email is the easiest and most efficient way to nurture leads, there are many other lead-nurturing options. Kristin explains, "You aren't limited to email. Have a team member reach out and make a phone call if you have a prospect's number. If you have a mailing address, send them paper invitations to events. Or even just send them a holiday card. If you have a niche that only communicates by text, send them a text."

The key is to tailor your lead nurturing so that everything you send adds value to the prospective client.

COMMUNITY: UTILIZE ADS

If you have the marketing budget to do so, use ads to expand the reach of your content. For example, you might promote your lead magnet or the content you are already posting on social media to a wider audience using paid advertisements, usually called "promoted" or "boosted" posts.

You may want to advertise in highly targeted niche publications and websites. The most common way to do this is in the form of advertorials. Advertorials are articles that you pay to place in publications. They look like native content, but in reality, they are paid ads. For advisors looking to be an expert in a niche, advertorials are a better use of money than standard image-based ads featuring your logo, a stock photo, a list of services, and your website. In my earlier example, the financial advisor focused on real estate agents pays a magazine to publish his article each month. This article has led to more awareness in his niche as well as event opportunities with the magazine.

If enough people are searching for your service on Google (e.g., financial advisor for dentists), you might consider using Google search ads. These ads allow you to bid on certain search terms people are searching for so that you turn up on Google results if your website is not organically ranking for those words. Ads can complement your SEO efforts in that you can turn up in Google results as you are building a strategy for your organic results.

Any of the advertising methods above require a budget in the thousands if not tens of thousands to implement. This is a good trade-off for those advisors who have more money than time to dedicate to their niche. The key to success is that your ads must be highly targeted to your niche with a message that resonates.

BUSINESS MODEL: ESTABLISH YOUR PROPRIETARY PROCESS

By year two, you should have enough experience to start developing a process specifically designed for your niche. Your proprietary process is the path that your company follows to achieve transformative results for your clients. Most financial advisors take their clients through a similar process: information gathering, goal setting, analysis and recommendation, implementation, and monitoring. Your proprietary process should customize this process to achieve results for your niche. This may mean adding in additional steps or just customizing the names of the process steps of the standard CFP Board's financial planning process to speak the language of your niche. Advisors with more control over their business will find this an easier task than employee advisors or enterprise RIAs.

ONE STEP AT A TIME

In the second year, you start to feel like an uncomparable financial advisor. You have taken all the activities of year one and added depth. As your ability to serve your niche becomes more sophisticated, so does your credibility as an expert. In Chapter 12, you will learn what to do in year three and beyond to succeed at a marketing strategy that prompts your ideal client to seek you out.

KEY TAKEAWAYS

- In the second year of your marketing strategy, you expand on your initial efforts from year one. Continue to get in front of your niche by being a guest everywhere you can (e.g., podcasts and presentations).

- At this stage, you truly are becoming an expert in your niche's needs. Use your insights and knowledge to expand on your content, and start optimizing it so more prospects can find you when they use Google and other search engines.

- Tend to your network by expanding on your efforts to nurture COIs and leads, and start using ads to get your firm in the public eye.

- Finally, after a year of experience with your niche, you will better understand how you should serve them. Use this understanding to establish your proprietary process.

CHAPTER 12

Year Three and Beyond

B y year three, you will see the rewards of your efforts, and you'll make refinements and additions that continue to propel your business forward into becoming uncomparable. The following activities are appropriate layers to start adding in year three (although you may find you wait until years four or five to implement them). In this case, I have added "optional" next to some of the activities because you are in no way required to implement all of them. In fact, of the optional items listed, I usually find firms generate more opportunities than they can handle using just one or two of these tactics. I suggest that instead of tackling all of them, choose the one that you are most passionate about doing.

NETWORK: HOST VIRTUAL OR IN-PERSON EVENTS (OPTIONAL)

Hosting your own events, whether online or virtual, requires a large email list to get people to attend. By year three, you should have been building your list to have enough people now that you can host an event of your own without relying on the networks of others. If you still don't have enough people to host your own event, consider partnering with another affiliated professional to do a joint event.

If your niche is primarily made up of local people, you can host live events. If your niche is nationwide, then do webinars or another virtual event.

If in doubt about your ability to pull off live events, my recommendation would be to lean toward virtual events. Live events require an incredible amount of time and money to execute. And on top of that, there is the added stress around if people show up or not and how that makes you look. A virtual event, on the other hand, takes less time, is less stressful, and can be repurposed for other content. It also provides you the flexibility to expand into non-local markets in the future without having to adapt your marketing plan.

However, I have seen enterprise RIAs implementing a multi-niche approach be wildly successful in hosting live niche events on a regular basis because of their large client base. The key to these events is to make them specific to your niche and their interests. Avoid generic topics that would appeal to any audience.

EXPERTISE: HOST A PODCAST (OPTIONAL)

Hosting a niche-focused podcast immediately positions you as an expert. It provides an opportunity to reach out to influential people in your niche community to be guests. And it provides an intimate way for prospects to get to know you. According to Matt Halloran of ProudMouth, the optimal show is twenty-six to twenty-eight minutes, released twice a month. He also observes that successful advisors he works with have been in their niche four to five years prior to starting their own show, so you may need to wait a few years before implementing this.

You can learn how to create your own podcast on YouTube, or I recommend the book *NPR's Podcast Start Up Guide: Create, Launch, and Grow a Podcast on Any Budget* by Glen Weldon. For most established firms, I recommend that you hire a freelancer or podcast agency to manage this process for you.

Podcasts are a major time and money investment. You have to consistently put out episodes, and once you start, it can be hard to stop. Make sure you are ready for this commitment before you start it.

EXPERTISE: WRITE A BOOK (OPTIONAL)

Writing a book can be the piece that finally propels you to the status of expert. By year three (or later), you should have plenty of experience working with your niche and likely have enough knowledge to write a book.

Books like AJ Harper's *Write a Must-Read: Craft a Book That Changes Lives—Including Your Own* and Rob Fitzpatrick and Adam Rosen's *Write Useful Books: A Modern Approach to Designing and Refining Recommendable Nonfiction* will give you ideas on how to use the book writing process to market your business long before the book is published. If you are interested in having a book but aren't interested in writing it, you can hire services that will do everything from writing the book to publishing it for you.

Once you have your book, give it away for free to everyone in your niche. You'll likely never earn back through book sales the money you invested, but it only takes a handful of clients resulting from the book to get the ROI you are looking for.

Use your book to leverage speaking engagements and podcast appearances as well as PR in your niche community. For Bruce Barton, our financial advisor to tech professionals, writing a book gave him a way to reach his niche.

"This niche, in particular, is hard to proactively reach. You can't call them on the phone. They don't answer. There's no way to reach people on the phone. And you can't send them mail."

When Bruce published his book, he now had something of value to offer his niche that they wouldn't immediately ignore. He paired his book with a social media strategy to start generating leads. "We've been using LinkedIn to reach out to this niche and offer free copies of the book," explains Bruce.

Bruce offers a copy of the book in exchange for their contact information. After they have received the book, prospects will often reach out to schedule a consultation. This system has been so effective for Bruce that it has been running consistently for three years without an end in sight.

COMMUNITY: SPONSOR EVENTS (OPTIONAL)

If there are events such as conferences or trade shows that attract your niche, this is the time to sponsor them or reserve a booth. This is by no means a requirement, though, and in fact, if you are consistently getting speaking engagements, you can probably skip this step altogether. But it can be a good way to show your niche that you are committed, engaged, and invested in their community.

Sponsoring events requires a budget usually in the tens of thousands of dollars. And once you sponsor one, you'll be continually asked to sponsor future events. If you are going to go down this path, it is something you should implement consistently, year over year, and probably over multiple events in a year.

NETWORK: ANALYZE YOUR CAMPAIGN FUNNELS

It is time to analyze your campaign funnels. By year three, you have a variety of campaigns you are implementing, such as blogs, podcasts, events, webinars, speaking engagements, etc. Chances are, you haven't taken the time to analyze the campaign funnel for each to determine if you are efficiently guiding a prospect from the stage of learning about your company to getting into your database to scheduling an appointment to becoming a client.

Kristin Harad recommends building a flow chart for every campaign you have, one that ensures there's always a flow to both the next piece of content they should consume and the next action they should take for working with you.

For every marketing asset you have, ask yourself these questions:

1. How would someone find this?

2. If I don't have their contact information, how would I get it from them?

3. What content would they be interested in next?

4. What action do I want them to do next if they want to work with me?

Let's illustrate this with an example.

ASSET: YOU HOST A GUEST-BASED
PODCAST TWICE A MONTH

1. **How would someone find the podcast?** My guests will promote it to their network via social media and email marketing. I will also be a guest on other podcasts

and promote my show. And I will promote on my own social media.

2. **If I don't have their contact information, how would I get it from them?** At the end of the show, I will direct them to a landing page on my website to provide their email address in exchange for downloading my eBook *Ten Things Every [Niche] Needs to Know to [Achieve This Benefit]*.

3. **What content would they be interested in next?** The eBook.

4. **What action do I want them to take next if they want to work with me?** At the end of the show, I will direct them to visit my website to schedule an introductory call.

Then you go through these same questions with any other assets mentioned in your answers.

ASSET: *TEN THINGS EVERY [NICHE] NEEDS TO KNOW TO [ACHIEVE THIS BENEFIT]* EBOOK

1. **How would someone find the eBook?** I promote it on my podcast and on the website.

2. **If I don't have their contact information, how would I get it from them?** Not applicable. If they have the eBook, I have their information.

3. **What content would they be interested in next?** An email series featuring one short video per email recapping each of the ten points in the eBook.

4. **What action do I want them to do next if they want to work with me?** At the end of the eBook, I will have a call to action to schedule an introductory call.

Even if you aren't sure how to design a campaign funnel, answering these questions will get you most of the way there.

Kristin sums it up this way, "The biggest service you can do for a potential client is to let them know what you want them to do next in your process. At the end of everything you send, always close with, 'And if you need help, this is what you do.' Or 'To take the next step, click here.' They should always know what the next action is that you want them to take."

POSITION: READDRESS YOUR BRAND

In the first year, I recommended changing only the images of your brand to reflect your niche. By year three or beyond, you may want to invest some money into rebranding your company to be completely tailored to the preferences of your niche. You may even want to consider changing the company name to reflect the niche. For my fictitious company serving commercial pilots, this would be the point when she changed the name from Esperanza Wealth Management to Aviation Capital Management. Of course, changing a company name should not be taken lightly and is only an option for solo practitioners and boutique RIAs that are specialized in only one niche.

COMMUNITY: CREATE YOUR OWN COMMUNITY (OPTIONAL)

Consider creating your own community within your niche, a place where people come to gather and talk about their shared interests.

For instance, you can start and facilitate a group for your niche on a social media site (e.g., a Facebook group for widows in your area). Or you can host community events such as a professional women's meetup group. Leading your own communities will position you as the ultimate influencer in the niche.

BUSINESS MODEL: CREATE A UNIQUE CLIENT EXPERIENCE

By the end of year three, you should be clear on whether or not you want to commit to your niche fully. If the answer is yes, this is the time to create a unique client experience. The client experience includes your office, staff, deliverables, and technology.

What type of office environment, if any, does your client want to visit? What skills do your staff need to have? What deliverables does your niche want to see? What special technology will best serve your niche?

For employee advisors and enterprise RIAs, you will be limited on the extent you can customize your client experience for your niche. But for everyone else, once you're ready to fully commit to your niche, it's time to start building your entire business around it.

NICHE: REFINE AND ADAPT

At this stage of your strategy, your focus is refinement. Do you need to narrow your niche or expand it? Do you need to redefine your client persona to include a higher-net-worth clientele? Do you need to update your messaging to reflect a narrower or expanded niche? This process never really ends since you will always be refining who your ideal niche client is.

AS YOU APPROACH THE JOURNEY'S END . . .

At this point, you have the Uncomparable Framework to build out, the strategies to focus on, and the knowledge to adapt for your firm type. So, how do you know if you are succeeding? In Chapter 13, you will learn what an uncomparable advisor does and does not do so you can adapt as necessary and succeed.

KEY TAKEAWAYS

- Year three and beyond provides opportunities to enhance your marketing strategy. You can host events either virtually or in person to build your network. You can also connect with your niche community by sponsoring events or creating your own community where your niche can congregate.

- Continue to focus on advancing your expertise. You can host a podcast where you invite influential people in your niche community to guest. Writing a book may be the ultimate in exhibiting your expertise, and just a handful of new clients can exceed your publishing expenses.

- Refinements will continue in your network (now is the time to determine how efficient your campaign funnels are) and your brand (perhaps including a name change to attract your niche).

- Finally, your business model activities can include customizing your client experience, so it directly serves your niche.

CHAPTER 13

Becoming Uncomparable

O ver the years, I have seen advisors succeed with a niche, and I have seen advisors fail with a niche. What makes one advisor succeed and another fail? **In my experience, uncomparable advisors share key traits: they keep their eyes on their goal, they are not easily distracted, they do the hard work, and they're willing to adapt as they go.**

Without these traits, a niche marketing strategy can easily dissipate. With these traits, an advisor can create a profitable firm that effortlessly attracts clients because there is nothing else like it.

This chapter explores those traits in more detail. It also discusses how to refine your niche, so you remain uncomparable, and it paints a picture of success to inspire you to stay the course. Let's start with the characteristics that uncomparable advisors must cultivate to succeed . . .

THE KEY TRAITS OF SUCCESSFUL ADVISORS

Commitment, Focus, and Persistence

One of the most common reasons why a niche doesn't work is because the advisor did not put in the time and effort needed to pursue it. I often observe advisors fearing to talk to people about what they do. They will hide behind blogging or using paid ads instead of taking the time to have one-on-one conversations with people (either online or offline). These advisors hope to have a landing page on their website and simply watch the leads come in.

I also see advisors fall back to generalist activities. If they don't see immediate success, they think what they are doing isn't working and go back to old habits. Remember, it takes three years for real success, so just keep working the plan. This uncomparable process takes time and effort, but the more activity you do on the front end, the quicker the payoff will be.

Not Chasing Random Acts of Marketing and Silver Bullets

Random acts of marketing are those "brilliant" ideas or shiny objects that are going to shift the trajectory of your marketing. Usually, these ideas come from a sales representative trying to sell you something, or they could come from a conference or webinar session designed to draw attendance.

While random acts of marketing sound good, they rarely produce results. When you implement random acts of marketing, you will

- Take time, money, and energy from the well-thought-out marketing strategy that took weeks, months, or even years to develop

- Make your staff members feel like they are chasing their tails

- Confuse the community, prospects, clients, and COIs over your messaging and branding

Niche marketing is all about focus and consistency, which means you may even have to power through when the marketing tactics you are implementing become boring to you. It's usually when you reach personal boredom that your marketing starts to sink in with your niche. It is critical not to get distracted by new and exciting things at every turn.

Similarly, a silver bullet ensuring easy success does not exist, and if it did, every other advisor would be using it. While eventually you will be able to automate or outsource a lot of tasks in your marketing system, you're never going to be able to just set it and forget it.

Not Outsourcing with Abandon

I see too many advisors who want to offload all their marketing responsibility to some third-party consultant or technology. Third parties can provide tremendous value to help you execute your marketing, but only you are responsible for your own firm's vision, strategy, and results. You must be highly engaged in this process if you expect it to work.

You can reasonably expect to outsource creative tasks such as ghostwriting, recording videos, coordinating and editing a podcast, optimizing your SEO, and designing a website. You can also outsource administrative-type tasks like posting a blog, sending a newsletter, coordinating events, or promoting company content on social media. But you have to set the vision and goals, nurture the most important relationships, be the thought leader, and drive results. No matter if you are an employee advisor or a business owner, you are the leader of this niche strategy, and you should only outsource support functions.

REFINING YOUR NICHE

When It Is Time to Niche Down

At some time in the first three years of your niche, or maybe even later, you may come to a point when it is time to narrow in even more—it's time to niche down. This may happen because competition has entered your market and you need to specialize even more to differentiate. Or maybe the niche you chose still has too many variations in their needs and you find there is a subset within the niche that you serve best.

For example, you work with business owners, but you add the most value to business owners in professional services. This is where you niche down and become more specific. You start working with consultants, accountants, and lawyers. This added specificity will help you stand out even more.

Cathy Curtis describes her journey to niching down to self-made women: "I was one of the first advisors to really focus on the financial needs of women. While we don't consider women a niche now, at the time, there were very few advisory firms that positioned themselves as woman-focused firm[s]. Today, the competition has flooded that market when they realized how much wealth women control in this country. I couldn't be different enough nearly by being woman-focused. I found I enjoyed working with successful single women or women who were the breadwinner in their family. They were all self-made, female-run households. So, I decided to narrow in on this group, and it has made all the difference in the growth of my business."

Niching down is an easier, more subtle process than picking a niche initially. You can revisit the steps in the six elements of the Uncomparable Framework and refine each step to reflect your new subset of clients.

When It Is Time to Niche Up

When I talk to advisors about niching, the conversation is usually about narrowing the niche to become more specialized. However, there may be times when it makes sense to expand your niche. For example, you may have dominated your market and need to expand just to continue growing your business. Or maybe your original niche is no longer viable, and you need to expand if you want to continue attracting new clients.

When you are ready to expand your niche, start by looking at markets that share a similar problem to your existing niche. For example, if you work with widows, you could expand into divorcees since both groups share the problem of being solely responsible for their household finances for the first time. Or if you work with tech employees, you could expand into biotech and pharma employees who share the problem of managing their equity compensation.

When I spoke with Lindsey Swanson, the financial advisor for legal sex workers, she expressed concern about government or internet regulations eventually prohibiting her from working with her clients. And she was planning for how she could adapt her business if and when this happens.

For Lindsey, she could probably expand into online influencers. These clients would share many of the issues as her existing clients, such as fluctuating income from an online business and a limited amount of time to be able to earn so much money.

If you find that it's time to expand, the key is to find a new market that shares the same problem as your existing niche. Then apply the same Uncomparable Framework to your new niche.

WHAT SUCCESS LOOKS LIKE

By now, you're likely ready to become uncomparable. Hopefully, you're excited and willing to put in the work over the next few years to get there. But you may be wondering what success looks like three years from now when you have implemented this strategy. Beyond the statistics I mentioned already from the 2020 Kitces.com study, I have found that advisors who niche also see the following benefits.

Marketing ROI

By focusing on a specific niche, you can tailor all of your marketing efforts toward reaching your ideal client and your ideal client only—maximizing your limited marketing dollars. While this will narrow your potential universe of prospects, it will deliver more qualified leads, resulting in a higher prospect-to-client conversion rate.

If you are successful in integrating yourself into a niche, you'll find that marketing will then take you less time and cost you less money than if you position yourself as a generalist. Your reputation spreads quickly. A lot of your marketing will come from word-of-mouth sources—not just from referrals but from people who are generally aware of you and your work but can't articulate how. This is because clients of similar situations and characteristics flock together.

Referral Generation

You will become known as the expert in working with your niche. Referrals from clients and centers of influence will increase because it's easier for them to make the connection between who you serve, the problems you can solve, and the overall value you bring to the table. You'll also receive referrals from other financial advisors.

Efficiency Gains

Rather than catering to numerous client segments, you can focus your efforts and staff on delivering one engaging client experience designed specifically around the needs, expectations, and complexities of your ideal client. When you have a niche, you have increased efficiencies in your business because the challenges your clients face are similar enough that you can streamline services, strategies, and solutions that apply to all of them. In other words, your business will be more scalable.

Your Happiness

Working with clients you are passionate about helping can go a long way toward increasing your personal satisfaction and happiness. When you successfully implement a niche strategy, every new client you work with is an ideal client and someone you enjoy working with. If you choose a niche that combines your interests with your expertise, you will find your work even more fulfilling.

This is what is possible when you become uncomparable.

Now, bring this into focus for yourself.

IMAGINE . . .

What will you be doing in three years?

Will you still compete with every other financial advisor in town for the same pre-retirees and retirees? Will your biggest differentiator be that you are a "fee-only, independent fiduciary" like so many others? Will you still be frustrated because the latest shiny market-ing trend turned out to be fool's gold, and so you reach for the next trend, and the next one, and on and on?

Or will you have broken out from the pack? Will you stand out to your niche community because no one else is helping them? Will you easily build your client base because you are an expert in your niche community? Do referrals come effortlessly because your clients and COIs trust you? Will you have the sweet gratification of knowing your knowledge is helping people live better lives?

Will you be incomparable or uncomparable? The choice is yours.

Acknowledgments

First and foremost, I want to thank Kari Helton. Without her help, the chapters in this book would have no transitions or conclusions. She has helped me clarify my writing for more than eight years, and her contribution to this book was invaluable.

I also want to thank Tracy Beckes and Vanessa Oligino, who have contributed both directly and indirectly to the concepts in this book over the years.

This book would not have made it through the various stages without my book coaching, support, editing, and publishing team, including Stacy Ennis, Robin Bethel, Gavin McMahon, and the River Grove team.

Thank you to all the niche financial advisors I've worked with over the years, especially those who lent their stories and insight to this book, including Bruce Barton, Cathy Curtis, Eric Sigdestad, Lindsey Swanson, Jane Mepham, Marlon Wesh, and Allen Giese.

I'd also like to thank financial services marketing experts Kristin Harad and Matt Halloran for the insights included in this book.

Many of the early ideas presented here were first published as initial drafts on Kitces.com and Advisor Perspectives. Thank you to Michael Kitces and Robert Huebscher for allowing me to flesh out my ideas to the readers of their publications.

I would like to thank my beta readers Ashley Gliss, Brian Peterson, Eric Courage, Mike Farrow, Rick Raybin, Evor Vattuone, Julie Bray, Corrinne McKenna, Jennifer Kirby, Jim Ludwick, Kelly Nilsson, Cleve Gantt, Vincent Florack, Don Hance, Jr., Brittany Fox, Chad Onufrechuk, Jessica McDonald, and Cathy Curtis.

Finally, I want to thank my partner, John Scott, and my mom, Nancy Luke, for listening to me talk about this book for over a year, even though they had no idea what I was talking about. Thank you for humoring me.

Further Reading

I'm an insatiable reader, so many of the thoughts in this book are an assimilation and evolution of the various books I have read over the years. While I quoted the sources I directly borrowed from, here is a list of books that have influenced this book in some way.

- *Become Known For A Niche You Own: Why Legendary Writers Use Languaging to Design New & Different Categories* by Category Pirates

- *The Thought Leader Formula: Strategically Leverage Your Expertise to Drive Business & Career Goals* by Robin Farmanfarmaian

- *The Paradox of Choice: Why More Is Less* by Barry Schwartz

- *The 1-Page Marketing Plan: Get New Customers, Make More Money, and Stand Out from the Crowd* by Allan Dib

- *The 12 Week Year: Get More Done in 12 Weeks Than Others Do in 12 Months* by Brian P. Moran

- *Selling the Invisible: A Field Guide to Modern Marketing* by Harry Beckwith

- *$100M Offers: How to Make Offers So Good People Feel* Stupid *Saying No* by Alex Hormozi

- *Get Different: Marketing That Can't Be Ignored!* by Mike Michalowicz

- *Niche Down: How to Become Legendary by Being Different* by Christopher Lochhead and Heather Clancy

- *Differentiate or Die: Survival in Our Era of Killer Competition* by Jack Trout

- *If You Want to Get Rich, Build a Power Niche: . . . and a Bundle of Other Utterly Brilliant Marketing & Sales Ideas That Actually Work* by Bruce M. Stachenfeld

- *Building a StoryBrand: Clarify Your Message So Customers Will Listen* by Donald Miller

- *The Business of Expertise: How Entrepreneurial Experts Convert Insight to Impact + Wealth* by David C. Baker

- *The Pumpkin Plan: A Simple Strategy to Grow a Remarkable Business in Any Field* by Mike Michalowicz

- *NPR's Podcast Start Up Guide: Create, Launch, and Grow a Podcast on Any Budget* by Glen Weldon

- *Write Useful Books: A Modern Approach to Designing and Refining Recommendable Nonfiction* by Rob Fitzpatrick and Adam Rosen

- *Write a Must-Read: Craft a Book That Changes Lives—Including Your Own* by AJ Harper

About the Author

KRISTEN LUKE is a marketing consultant who helps registered investment advisors and their employees market themselves to a niche, making it easier for them to stand out from the competition and attract ideal clients.

She has dedicated her career to learning the ins and outs of financial advisor marketing. Since starting her career in the industry in 2005, she has worked with hundreds of financial advisors to easily generate leads so they can quit worrying about marketing and get back to focusing on the areas of their businesses they enjoy.

Kristen frequently shares her marketing expertise at industry events and in podcasts and publications.

Kristen holds her private pilot license for single-engine aircraft and her instrument rating. She splits her time between her home in San Diego, California, and her cabin in Idyllwild, California.

Made in the USA
Monee, IL
31 July 2023

40248958R00125